M000033288

## Dedication

**To BIGGIE. That's his nickname. It stands for Bare-chested Internet Guru.**

**We meet twice weekly over Skype since he lives in Costa Rica, and he (almost) never wears shirts! His other name is Micah Guller; he's my IT genius and Marketing Master. The Daily Dose was his idea. And it was a brilliant one.**

**So thank you, BIGGIE, for your creative genius, for your incredible availability, service and most importantly, your friendship.**

# Preface

As I mentioned in the dedication, the Daily Dose wasn't my idea. It was the idea of my marketing and IT genius, Micah Guller. The full title of it is, The Daily Dose: Mental Toughness Tips in 30 Seconds or Less. It's an email that goes out every morning with the intention of helping you get your mind right as soon as you awaken so that you can not only win the day, but also strengthen your mind permanently in the process and develop more Mental Toughness that will help you live more happily and more powerfully.

This book is a collection of the first 365 Daily Dose messages. Use it however you deem valuable. Maybe it's like a calendar where the first entry is for January 1. Or maybe you'll prefer to open up "randomly" to some page and see what the message is that the Universe thought relevant for you that day.

In any case, I STRONGLY recommend that you don't just read these messages, but rather that you USE these messages. Read just one a day. Then after reading it, let it settle for a moment, see if it resonates with you. And if it does, then ask yourself, "How can I integrate this and utilize this today in order to be more joyful or powerful or compassionate or successful?" Use these Daily Doses as tools for growth. That's they're meant for.

Additionally, you will notice that some of the Daily Doses are repetitive, or even close to identical. That's actually a great thing. I don't ever look back at what I've already written as I sit to compose more of the doses. I actually don't care if they're redundant. Or, rather, I DO care. I LIKE that some are redundant, because there's great value in the repetition. That's how Mental Toughness Training works. Reps. So, when you notice some repetition, be enthused.

My intention for both the email list as well as this book is the same: to help spread awareness of the value of investing in strengthening your mind so that you experience life miraculously.

Create Miracles!

Love, Chris

If you aren't already on the <u>email list</u>
for The Daily Dose, I highly recommend that
you sign up.

# Sign Up at This Link Below
## https://christopherdorris.com/dd

… we've had a few days this first year when
The Daily Dose did not go out as planned, and
each time I got emails from folks asking what
happened, wanting to make sure that I was
still doing it and that they were still on the list!

This list is only for serving YOU.

There will not be ANY marketing messages
sent out via this list. Not by me, not by anyone.
I also hate SPAM and will never sell, rent, lend
or share your information with anyone.

I have thoughts, but I am not my thoughts.

Become a slightly skeptical observer of the content of your mind and ask yourself, "do I believe what I'm thinking?"

Ain't Bad; Just Is.

It's one of my favorite mantras. I want my lowest
interpretation of reality to be neutral.
When you catch yourself complaining,
this is a good replacement thought.

You are infinite possibilities.

Really. When you were born you were doubtless. And you were experiencing reality as a field of infinite possibilities.

Be that way again today.

Do you have anything important going on today or coming up soon?

Prepare mentally for it by envisioning complete success beforehand. And do it in detail.

You're pre-programming yourself to crush it.

**Got your Game Face on today?**

**Don't know exactly what it is? I got your back. What do you FEEL like (emotionally) when you're at your best? Answer that.**

**That's your Game Face. Recreate that state!**

Start the day off with enthusiasm.

The word comes from the Greek entheos, which means creator within. What are you enthused about? Think about it. When you do, you release serotonin and dopamine. They are the "ON switches" for all intelligence centers of the brain.

Feel great AND activate!

What are you waiting for???

Waiting is the #1 mistake I witness people making in the pursuit of the lives of their dreams.

Make a commitment to do something bold today that you've been waiting on!

Einstein said, "There are only two ways to see the world. One is as if nothing is a miracle. The other is as if everything is."

See the miracles today.

You are what your deepest desire is.

As is your desire, so is your intention.
As is your intention, so is your will.
As is your will, so is your deed.
As is your deed, so is your destiny.

- Upanishads (Ancient Vedic Text)

There's this great saying that goes:

*"The pessimist complains about the wind, the optimist is sure it'll go away, whereas the realist simply adjusts the sails and flies across the sea."*

The point is, both the pessimist AND the optimist have a problem with reality. They both interpret the wind as an inconvenience.

Only the realist (someone who chooses to experience reality opportunistically) can see the potential value in every moment.

So, most often when someone says, "I'm not a pessimist, I'm just a realist!" that means they are a pessimist pretending to be a realist.

Be a realist today. Practice working WITH reality.

The "HOW" is in the "WHAT."

In other words, inherent within your desires (the "what") are the mechanics for their own fulfillment.

So don't hesitate if you can't see the HOW.

Just move towards.

**One of my favorite
definitions of enlightenment is this:**

**"The ability to choose peace amidst chaos."**

**Go ahead and do that today.**

There's no such thing as "failure" - there are only results. And all results are valuable.

When I get what I want, I get to celebrate.

When I don't, I get to grow.

Create the state - don't wait.

Which state? Well, whichever one is going to serve you in the moment. You choose your states with your thought content.

Choose wisely today.

The outer world is a reflection of the inner world.

So what you have going on in your life is the result of what you've got going on in your mind.

Strengthen the content.

Stay above the O-Line today. That's the observation line. The three ways we interpret reality all day are: low grade, neutral (observation, or O-Line) and high grade.

Practice catching yourself below the O-Line and then upgrading your thinking.

Every set of circumstances can be leveraged for individual and collective gain if viewed masterfully. View masterfully today.

I use history,
but I don't permit history to use me.

I love that mantra. History is simply a memory. A thought. And thus, it can be thought of however you please - or however will most likely have you be amazing.

So be very selective with what you choose to recall, AND recall it in ways that will increase the likelihood of activating your badassery.

Yes, that's permissable.
And it's free. Happy Day!

**Do you really need anything in particular to happen today in order to decide that it's the best day of your life?**

*"I embrace uncertainty, paradox and ambiguity."*

**Have that be your mantra for today.**

Here's one we'd all do well to remember today - before you speak, ask yourself:

*"Is it true? Is it necessary? Is it kind?"*

If no is the answer to any, redirect.

The difference between a goal and a decision
is that a goal leaves the door open
for the possibility of failure,
whereas a decision does not.

What might you be settling for?

In the complete privacy of your own mind, ask yourself that, and answer it.

And then make a bold move today. Yeah, Baby!

Gratitude is one of the most intelligent states we could ever choose to think our way into (see the language I used there?).

Practice gratitude a lot today.

Remember some of your greatest successes from the past seven days. Re-experience them in your mind's eye. Burn those into your neural network.

Another one of my favorite definitions of enlightenment is this: having a mind that is open to everything and attached to nothing.

That's real freedom, isn't it?

I am open to miracles, and am simultaneously cool with whatever unfolds. Can't lose.

My main man, Carl Jung often referred to "the shadow" as the part of our personalities that have yet to be brought into the light of consciousness.

A shadow can't exist when you shine light onto it.

Today, pay attention to your moods.
With lightness. Simply observe.

Have you ever tried Transcendental Meditation?

It's pretty bad ass.

Tons of benefits to practicing it. It's really unique because it involves letting the thought pumping part of the brain take a load off.

Give it a whirl.

See if you can at least permit yourself to slow your thoughts by simply not giving a damn about the activity of your mind for several minutes.

See how you feel afterwards.

In the ancient language, Sanskrit, there's a phrase, Tat Tvam Asi. Loosely translated, it means, "That Thou Are." It's a reminder to practice remembering that we are all connected at the most fundamental, energetic level.

Today, practice noticing sameness.

My all time favorite definition of enlightenment
came from my dasa ji (my teacher) at
The Oneness University in India.

We were just hanging out one evening after the
lectures and exercises and meditations were
over and I asked her,
"How do YOU define enlightenment?"

So she went silent, smiling,
for about 45 seconds, and then said:
"Having no internal conflict."

All results fall into one of two categories:

(A) You got what you wanted.

(B) You didn't.

And both are exactly equally valuable (if you'll see them the right way).

When you get what you want, you get to celebrate and enjoy what you created. When you don't get what you want, you get to grow.

We can ONLY grow with strain, and as humans, we're designed for growth.

So in that light, you can't lose.

A great practice I learned in one of the Deepak Chopra retreats I attended was this:

For today, practice replacing acknowledging how different you are from others with recognizing SAMENESS.

It's a complete energetic shift. Play with that.

Relinquish the need to defend.

Today you might notice if and when you get defensive. Just notice it. With light-heartedness.

Then ask yourself, "What was I defending?"

Question for you:

What percentage of your life do you spend in a
state of wishing things were different?

Today you might experiment with decreasing
that percentage and instead spend more time in
states like gratitude and enthusiasm.

And witness how much more creativity
you bring to "problem" solving.

No one really wants to hurt anyone else.

The only reason we hurt others is because of our own unhealed pain. Remembering that helps me lose the shame I put on myself when I hurt another, and it helps me not take it personally when someone acts hurtful towards me.

One of our greatest barriers to success
(having your life on your terms)
is what I call "The How Obstacle."

My friend and genius, Bill Girruzzi, writes, in
his epic paper, "Solving The Unsolvable:
Transforming the World in 25 Years or Less"
that the HOW can be all consuming because
the HOW is where our cynicism arises.

Here's a fun mantra for the day:

"Be willing to be wrong." We have been so heavily conditioned to believe how critical it is to be right.

Surrender that today. Take a load off.

See how many times today you can catch yourself being WRONG! And smile about it.

When you love what is,
what is is what you want.

Today let's both practice the art of Wu Wei,
or working with. Let's meet what comes
our way today with non-resistance,
like water flowing around a rock.

Today, when things go other than how you wanted them to, ask yourself two questions:

1) What's the learning in this?

2) And what good can I create from this?

Joseph Campbell used to always say, "Follow Your Bliss." And I positively love that.

Bliss is way high on the emotional spectrum. Good vibes. High vibrational state.

From those states come brilliance and creativity and excellence.

Came up with this little ditty earlier this morning:

"When you're feeling unpleasant,
you're simply not present."

But that's only true always. Think about it.

Disappointment and resentment come from me
ruminating about the past. And fear exists entirely
in future thinking.

So the present is pleasant. Simple as that.

**Do you have a Success Story file?**

There is so much value in keeping close track of your bad-assery. Don't brush off the amazing feedback that you get.
Instead, CAPTURE it.

And revisit it. Not to feed your ego, but rather to remind yourself of your power, influence, brilliance and impact.

The world needs you to remember that.

Today, be mindful of your yeses.

In fact, experiment with being stingy with them.
Exericse your "No Muscle" today.

And remember that "No." is a complete sentence.

**Heighten your awareness to your complaints.**

**Complaining, by definition, is a low grade interpretation of reality. And it deactivates intelligence. So, basically, it's stupid.**

**Catch yourself complaining and replace with expressions of gratitude.**

The whole process of mastering one's moods is contingent upon noticing them in the first place.

Ask yourself throughout the day, "What's my mood right now?" And label it. That's all.

Strengthen your ability to identify your states today, just a bit. "How am I feeling right now? I'm kind of irritated." Just from acknowledging it, you've transcended it - even if for only a moment.

You can only be governed by your moods when you're unaware of them.

Do you know that YOU are
an incomprehensible improbability?

Another way of saying that...
you're a miracle.
That's a mathematical fact.

The odds of you happening
are 1 in 10 to the 2.7 millionth power.
Celebrate that today!

Here's a fun paradox for you today...

The only thing we can be sure of is uncertainty.

We live in an uncertain universe. So our options are, (A) struggle against that, or (B) work WITH that. See if you can actually love the uncertainty you often worry about.

Is it possible that you could enjoy the not knowing? Like going to see a movie for the first time.

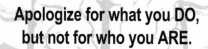

**Apologize for what you DO,
but not for who you ARE.**

I have this amazing client named Alan. He's an inventor. So every day he fails. A lot.

He tries, he fails. He tries, he fails. He tries, he fails. (Do that about 997 more times).

Then he tries one day and he succeeds.

And it's perfect.

Here's a GREAT Mental Toughness Tip:

Replace your "have to's" with "get to" and see if you can mean it.

That's a legit exercise. Serious game changer.

Nervous can't exist In Service.

It seems to be consistently true. I give a lot of talks and sometimes before the big ones, I get nervous. And then I remember that my nervousness is purely egocentric.

I'm deluding myself into believing that this event is about me, and doing good, and all that crap. When I am able to remember that I'm here as a servant, to deliver a gift, the nervousness transforms into serenity and even enthusiasm.

Who can you serve today?

I want my lowest grade interpretation
of reality to be an observation.

"Oh, whattaya know? My car's been stolen."
Not, "Holy shit! Someone stole my damn car!!!
This totally SUCKS!!!"

It actually doesn't suck at all.
And it isn't amazing either. Unless it is.
Which is up to me. And why would I want to
interpret that as amazing?

My only response to that is that when I'm
enthused, I'm smarter, more creative and happier.

And since I have equal access to misery and joy,
it seems to make sense to choose the latter.

Do you also suffer from T.A.N.E.?
The Addiction to Not Enough?

We have been conditioned to believe that our lives, precisely as they are in this very moment, are inadequate, and we experience a perpetual sense of internal conflict, or dis-ease.

We are urgently, desperately, frighteningly, driven to achieve more, to work harder, to make more money, to gain more respect, to get more recognition, bigger and better titles, bigger and better houses, and so on. And the source of that drive is almost always a complete illusion.

And the illusion is this: I am not enough.

How would you show up today, and how would you feel today, if you could remember that not only are you "enough", but also that you are EXACTLY where you need to be?

Do you know that puzzles are really good for your brain? All kinds of puzzles.

Doing puzzles is a great form of brain training. It significantly reduces the likelihood of certain neurological disorders. Puzzle on, Puzzler!

You know how sometimes people say things like, "That guy really pushes my buttons!"? Well, don't ever say stupid stuff like that. Because it's never EVER true. And it's weak.

"He" can't make you feel anything. The most "he" can do is act and speak in ways that make it easy for you to think yourself into being offended.

What's the best way to ensure that no one ever "pushes your buttons" again? Remove them.

I used to watch Star Trek: The Next Generation.

Lieutenant Commander Data, the android,
always fascinated me because he
wasn't able to feel emotions.

Not being able to feel emotions sounds sucky.
But the cool thing about it was that he was
always capable of seeing through the emotional
cloud to the relevant "data", or solution.

So there's something for us
to learn from him, isn't there?

Here's a little ditty for your day today...

"When you're feeling unpleasant,
you're simply not present."

Today (as I write this) marks the 7th anniversary
of me returning to my non-smoking status.

I stopped at midnight that day
and have never had an urge to smoke
a single cigarette since then.

Not one urge. You know why?

I took two full months to get ALL IN! in
advance and prepared myself psychologically,
thoroughly, every day, with enthusiasm.

I didn't "try" to quit.

I made a DECISION
to return to my non-smoking, healthy, pink lung
status, picked a date, recommitted 100 times
every day for two months, and thus there was
no chance of it not happening.

What do you want to get ALL IN! with?

Dedication is an incredible source of inspiration and power.

Dedicate today to someone you love and do everything today with that person in mind.

Let your love for them and their welfare be your driver.

I have a new mantra these days,
and I just love it!

*"Do It Anyway."*

I don't need to wait for the motivation to write
another chapter for the next book, or to record a
new video blog or craft another month of these
Daily Dose messages.

Even if I don't feel like it, I can just Do It Anyway.

Keep that in mind today.

No one makes you angry.

No one makes you happy.

You do that all on your own with
the way you think.

Exercise the freedom to
create your states mindfully today.

Do it more than yesterday.
And again tomorrow. And so on.

Today, practice converting adversity into fuel.
That's what the Mentally Tough do.
Like psychological alchemists.
Turning everything into gold.

Byron Katie (one of my fav teachers) says,
"Until you can look at all aspects of life without
fear, your work is not done."

So, today let's practice choosing
enthusiasm as our default response.

Here's a deep one for ya today. It's a fun mantra that I use in the beginning of my meditations.

"I am instantly and inextricably connected to all that exists across space-time."

Interesting how that was proposed thousands of years ago by the rishis and is now being supported by modern physics.

Feel connected today.

Interpreting something as an inconvenience is simply one (weak) way of seeing things.

It's weak because it doesn't lead to activation of creative genius or any form of intelligence.

Catch yourself today when you're thinking of things as "inconvenient" and see if you can turn that around into, at minimum, an interesting thing, or better yet, a blessing.

I wish I wasn't wishing shit was different.

See what I did there?

With light-heartedness (as always),
pay attention today
to the amount of time you spend
in a state of wishing things were different.

Billy Shakes (aka William Shakespeare) said, "Nothing good or bad happens until you think it so." So until we interpret things, they just ARE. Is-ness. Ain't bad; just is. unless it's good. Up to you.

Rather than complaining today, consider the possibility of a more functional approach to responding to the things that you initially wish were different.

Toy with the possibility that you can create something quite useful out of those situations - something that couldn't have been possibile if not for the "problem" itself.

Today say "Yes" and "Good" a lot. They're like multi-vitamins for the brain.

**As far as your emotions go,
I don't care WHAT you choose,
I care THAT you choose.**

It happened again today in a coaching call. Someone told me they were afraid that their expectations were too high.

That can never be true. Mathematically, we are miracles, so why not expect miracles?

As a child I was so blessed that
my family went to Disney World each year
between Christmas and New Years.

And I will never forget my spirit
as I pushed through the turnstyle
to enter The Magic Kingdom.
Enthusiasm and anticipation. Sheer joy.

What if the entire world was
our Magic Kingdom?

I really should stop saying "I should" so much.

We've learned to prioritize being liked and pleasing people over being honest.

As always, with lightness of being, today pay particular attention to when you may be betraying your truth.

There is no such thing as failure. There are only results. And there are two categories of results: (a) you got what you wanted, (b) you didn't.

Both are equally valuable.

When you get what you want , you get to celebrate and enjoy that. When you don't, you get to grow.

And we're designed for growth.

So thank goodness for the times when we don't get what we want!

"Stress Management" is so stupid.

We create every ounce of stress that we ever experience with low grade interpretations of reality. Fact. Indisputable.

Stress is entirely the result of choosing to think about the future disasterously. So we are 100% responsible for CREATING ALL OF OUR STRESS.

So explain me this: why in the hell would I ever want to "manage" an unpleasant thing that I totally create? Wouldn't I rather REMOVE it?

Yes. WE would prefer that.

So today (and forever more) catch yourself when you're feeling stressed, then immediately think your way into a state of gratitude.

Right out of college I impulsively took a job on a Scalloping Boat (that's what Pysch majors from the Jersey Shore do).

I worked 18 hour shifts in rough seas. In November. On a boat full of drug abusing yahoos.

Picking the big scallops out of the huge pile of creatures and trash we'd just drug up off the sea floor. IT SUCKED! Until it didn't.

And it starting not sucking when I stopped complaining about the situation and instead created a game out of it. I made a game out of how fast I could fill a bucket without getting bitten by a crab or some pissed off fish.

Making games out of tough tasks is a good tool.

**It never ceases to amaze me how much more free shit I get when I'm really kind to people.**

Pain is inevitable; suffering is optional.
Suffering comes from judging the pain as bad.

Shame is possibly the most toxic of all human emotions. And it's entirely unnecessary to carry around with you in life.

Just like a US President is entitled to grant "pardons" at the end of their term, without ANY justification whatsoever, so can you.

Pardon you. That simple. Pardon on!

Urgency is the "Need To" approach and Desire is the "Get To" approach to getting shit done. Both can inspire some profound action.

But, in the long run, one is FAR more productive than the other. I bet you can guess which.

Today, remind yourself to catch yourself when you are thinking about all the stuff you think you "need" to get done, and upgrade that thinking to "I get to!"

My client, Alan, is a phenomenal pianist.
And he said something recently that I just love.

He said, "In order to really masterfully
play a piece of music, you must first
be able to play it in your head."

Think about how many other things that can
apply to in your life...

A backhand heater in tennis.
A 2 yard draw in golf.
A slaes presentation.
Serving a customer or client.
Responding masterfully to a challenge.

The power of imagery is immense.
Use some today.

There are several messages in these Daily Doses that are somewhat redundant because they really bear repeating, and this is one of them.

STOP COMPLAINING!

It simply deactivates all forms of intelligence and forbids you from accessing your natural creative genius. We'll revisit this next month. ;)

One of the simplest and most powerful practices in upgrading your state and relaxing your body is breathing. We've all heard this a million times. This your millionth and one.

Breathe deeply right now.

You just oxygenated your bloodstream and relaxed your muscles.

Do that more.

If you're feeling guilty about something you're blowing off doing, then you're not blowing it off well enough.

If you're gonna blow it off, do it like a champ! If you aren't willing to do that, then just get up and go do the damn thing.

It's either "HELL NO!" or "HELL YEAH!"
But it ain't gonna be "hell maybe."

Here's a fun practice
for you to experiment with today.

Play with silence.

For example,
as you converse with people today,
let there be some silence
before responding.

Maybe just make eye contact and
let them begin the dialog.

Pay attention to the gaps between your words,
even. This is very disciplined.

We've been conditioned to fill the spaces with
noise. Explore the stillness of silence.

Break the pattern of noisiness a bit today.

Here's the "Post-Game" Routine I use with all my clients after they have a performance of any kind (it's so simple and powerful).

Answer the following 3 questions:

1) How was I amazing?
2) What's the one big lesson for me from this?
3) What, specifically, will I do to grow from it?

Try it out. Write them down and keep them together so you can look at them later on.

If you're in a leadership role, here's a valuable nugget from my late mentor, Jim Myers.

If you have someone on your team that you truly cannot get yourself to believe in, invite them into their futures ASAP. It's selfish of you to do otherwise. And terrible for your business.

You know what really stresses me out?

Can you guess?

Nothing. Except my shitty thinking.

There are no stressful events. That's a fact. Not a twist or a view through rose colored glasses. That's the view you get when you remove the glasses that would have you see the world problematically in the first place.

Feeling stressed? Upgrade your thoughts.

**When you love what is, what is is what you want.
With the right mindset, you can't lose.**

Every day, all day, you're having a
continuous internal dialog with yourself,
whether you know it or not.

And the content of
that dialog becomes the content of the images
you create in your mind. And the content of
those images become your outer world.

We would all do well to strengthen the content of
our inner world. Will you please do that today?

I'm a big fan of the power of full commitment, or as I like to call it, being ALL IN!

One of the remarkably unique distinctions about being ALL IN! versus any other lesser level of commitment is that when I'm ALL IN!, I never feel self-conscious about declaring to the world what I'm up to, what I'm creating. ALL IN!-ness is characterized by "Declaration without Hesitation!"

Today, create an opportunity to tell someone, anyone, about something bold that you're creating right now in your life.

Right now, I'm in a month-long practice of pattern interruption. I do this every year.

I take a month and examine my routines. I really examine them. And I ask myself, which ones serve me, which ones don't. How can I strengthen the ones that do? And let's modify or even delete the ones that don't. It's a great tune-up that helps to ensure I'm living more on-purpose.

For starters, today, simply pay attention to the different routines you have in place.

Morning routine.
Driving to work routine.
Work routine.
Lunch routine, etc.

Simply examine them with light-hearted curiosity.

Inherent within your desires are the mechanics for their own fulfillment.

"How the hell am I going to be able to do that?" Useless question.

Move towards your desire and activate the mechanics of its realization. Not fluff. Bad ass shit.

Read The Alchemist.

What if you TOTALLY changed your story to something like, "I LOVE discomfort so much so that I seek it out daily in an effort to ensure that not one day of my life passes during which I don't experience some amazing growth or personal development!"???

**A weak mind sees problems and complains about them. A Tough Mind sees opportunities and capitalizes upon them.**

**It's impossible to know that something is impossible. Right? Today, if you have the notion that something you desire is outside the realm of possibility, challenge that thought.**

Here's another of my favorite mantras:

"The nature of commitment is...
that it goes away."

Just like everything else in the universe,
commitment is impermanent. Which is perfectly
cool. Because we can always recommit.
Whenever we want.

So, today's suggestion is to think about
what in your life is it time to recommit to.

When we come into this life, we have yet to be educated about our limitations. Our default mentality is abundance. The world is a field of infinite possibilities. We can't even entertain "failure" because we don't know what the hell it is! That's our natural state.

So, let nothing ever have you call into question your excellence.

Great mantra:

"The nature of commitment is that it goes away."

Commitment has a short shelf life. So all that means is that - with the things that matter most to us - we need to recommit, or get ALL IN! Daily! As if for the first time.

Recommit to something big this morning.

Pain is inevitable; suffering is optional.

The difference is that I suffer when I judge the emotional pain. If I can simply experience the sadness, for example, without saying to myself, "This sucks" then it ain't bad. In fact it's kinda sweet.

Just for fun (which is purely intelligent),
what's something you could do today that will
have you feel more ALIVE and vibrant than you
did yesterday? Maybe something a bit bold.

What you got?

Learned limiting beliefs would have
most adults never even take the time
to sit for one hour of their lives
and reflect upon the question,
"How do I most profoundly want to use
the rest of my life?" And that's only the first step.

Once you have clarity, take immediate and bold
action. And take it from a place of fun and
certainty. And adjust the sails as you go.

It's the ultimate game of creation!

Ali Binazir of Harvard Mathematics calculated the odds of any one of us ever occurring.

It's literally mind boggling.

You are a 1 in 10 to the 2.7 millionth power probability. You got that?

That's like this: give 2 million people one die each that contains the numbers 1 through 1 trillion on it, have them all cast their dice and they ALL come up the same number. Cha Ching! Winner winner chicken dinner! Party on.

Billy Shakespeare said, "Nothing good or bad happens, until you think it so."

So, everything just is. Is. Until we interpret it.

And all research shows that when we interpret things in ways that have us be inspired, we release the neurotransmitters dopamine and serotonin - the "on switches" for all intelligence centers of the brain. In other words, we become bad ass.

So it's just smart to see the world in an inspired way. Your call.

Working with one of my competitive golf clients today on remembering how to love putting, I was reminded (RE-MINDED) that as children we instinctively experience life enthusiastically. Until we are taught to see life problematically.

But, we can train ourselves to get back to our enthusiastic and inspired experience of life. And that's some bad ass news!!!

We naturally experience reality
in an awe-inspired way. That's our default.
Until we are influenced by the world
to experience it problematically.

Here's the great news: with a little effort, we can
reprogram ourselves to see the world through
inspired lenses and feel awe and bewilderment
and gratitude and enthusiasm and collaboration
and cooperation and peacefulness. It seems like
that is what we are designed for.

I studied Astrophysics for a hot minute after college. Biggest lesson learned from that year of study: we don't just live in, but are part of, a universe that operates on a flawless operating system. Celebrate that today!

Complaining releases neurotransmitters
that make you stupid. Period.

"You're out of your mind!" is a fine compliment.
If it's accurate. In fact, it's remarkably difficult to
get out of mind, or out of thought - on purpose.

In sports, we refer to it as
The Zone = Thoughtless Perfection.
And it's oh so sweet.

Google "Getting in The Gap" and practice it.
The Beatles' guru, Maharishi Mahesh Yogi made
transcendental meditation a thing for bad asses.

Rock The Gap.

**YOU GOT THIS!!!!**

**Whatever your "this" is,
you got it.**

**I truly believe that by virtue of you being able to
even envision it, it's available to you in some form.**

**Move towards. Miracle on.**

Several years ago I was working with
a healer who taught me the practice of
"Radical Acceptance." Radical.

Not moderate. Not sorta kinda. But RADICAL!
Imagine your life when you have no self criticism.

If I can completely forgive myself,
then I'm free to truly spread love.

The practice of freeing ourselves from the conditioning of our pasts permits us to experience reality AS IT IS. Which is bad ass.

So today, do some inner strengthening by really paying attention to your moods. Label them as you catch them. And see if you can elevate them by altering your thinking in those moments.

Follow your bliss. Can't think of a more powerful three word piece of advice. Truly. My late mentor, Jim Myers, had a wood carving on his desk that read: Follow Your Bliss. It's consistent with all human peak performance research. The better we feel = the better we are. At everything. Ask really old people. They'll confirm it. And they know. They get it.

I am never late. Ever.

I set my alarm clock a little ahead. So when I wake up I think it's a little later than it is. Helps me be punctual. Helps me keep my word. It's a lie.

I'm deluding myself into thinking something is true that simply isn't. And it's smart. I'm happy to lie to myself if it helps me be powerful.

When I'm in that unique mood I'm in after I pull off something bad ass, I'm releasing the smart neurotransmitters. The "on switches" so to speak, of all the brain's intelligence centers. I'm activating creative genius. So instead of waiting for some bad ass accomplishment in order to feel that way, start by creating that state intentionally and THEN go get busy creating miracles to go celebrate!!!

When you love what is, what is is what you want.
Reality is perfect. It's our low grade interpretations
of it that are problematic. #enlightenup

When I was a Clinical Social Worker, working with the homeless, one of the most powerful observations I made was that the folks who refused to act like victims were the ones who seemed to get the "good breaks". Coincidence?

Entitlement is 100% victim thinking and thus weak. We create our lives. Own that.

ALL IN! is the state of infinite commitment. In that state, the possibility of "failure" is nonexistent in your field of consciousness.

You're so busy doing what it takes to get the thing done that you can't even contemplate the possibility of not. And that's as powerful as we get. BUT, there's a hitch. The nature of such commitment is that it goes away.

The shelf life of ALL IN!-ness is very brief. So we need to recommit daily, as if for the first time.

Then we crush. #allin!

I never want to trust my thoughts.
At least not the ones that have me feel like crap.

Whenever I'm feeling down, ever, it's only because in that moment I'm entertaining a thought that is simply not true.

I want to practice letting those thoughts go.
Do that more today please.

In Mental Toughness Training, the term "Game Face" refers to the mood you're in when you're at your absolute best.

When I'm coaching a committed athlete or executive, we spend enormous amounts of time utilizing classical conditioning techniques to create an "on switch" to that peak performance state so that the athlete/exec can turn it on in a hot second!!! And crush!!!

What is YOUR Game face?

How would you describe your mood when you're performing at peak?

The truth of the matter is, the only limitation we have is the belief that we have a limitation. And the good news is, we can discard that belief.

Can there be a greater roadblock to peace and compassion than the need for significance?

My desire for significance inspires me to prioritize being "right" and "recognized" over being loving and supportive. When I feel completely significant, on the deepest of possible levels, I have nothing but lightness and joy and peace and love to offer.

So, today (and forever if you feel like it) remember that you are an expression of Divine Grace in human form. You are a miracle. You couldn't possibly be more significant!

I just noticed something pretty cool. It's the word "humankind." It means the collective human race. And it could be like a math equation. Human + Kind = ??? What would you say that equates to?

Or what if we made it a multiplication equation? Human x Kind = ???

So, you're the human constant in the equation. The variable is kindness.

Mental Toughness is about choosing high grade emotions or states, like compassion and kindness.

Play around with upgrading your typical level of human-kindness and let's see what kind of good math we can all collectively create today!

Consciousness occurs AFTER the event.
Awareness occurs DURING it.

You can't push awareness. The more conscious
we become, the more capable we are of becoming
aware. Which is why I rely so heavily in my Mental
Toughness Coaching upon tools like the Post-
Game Analysis, and Imaginary "Do-Overs."

After a conversation, I can look back at it with
light-hearted curiosity and ask myself,

"How'd I do there? Was I honest? Was I bold?
Was I defensive? Was I present? Did I listen?
Was I prioritizing being right?
If I was going to have that conversation again,
might I speak or listen differently?"

And what I learn from these inquiries, raises my
consciousness. And that leads to being more
aware the next time.

A simple yet profound (again, my favorite combo) practice to experiment with today:

Respond to each situation where you don't get what you wanted with the question, "What can I create out of exactly this?"

Are you one of the many of us that waits until our backs are against the wall before you get uber determined and deliver?

If so, think about who and how you are when you're crushing it, write that down, start telling yourself 100 times per day that from now on you ARE THAT PERSON, and stop waiting for stuff to get hairy before you show up!

A prerequisite of true success is that you determine the role that YOU want money to play in your life. Otherwise you never succeed (no matter how much money you make) because money will own you forever.

Here's a good exercise that you can practice anywhere that'll help you get into the present moment: look around and don't interpret. Just look. See colors, shapes, shadows, textures. Simply be aware of the silent presence of the things you see.

Today practice noticing mutually exclusive assumptions and challenge them.

For example, the pathetic phrase, "No pain - no gain." Another faulty mutually exclusive ASSumption is, "Nice guys finish last."

See if you can catch yourself thinking of any of these or hear someone else uttering them, and challenge them in your mind.

80% of Americans report disliking their jobs.

That's disturbing. Let's flip that so that 80+% report being madly IN LOVE with their vocations.

Let's make it hugely unpopular to settle.

Mentally tough people understand the value of being an incredible listener.

So today, as you're listening to people speak, notice all the conclusions you come to as they're speaking. Discard them. And listen. Until the person is done.

Pause a moment.

Then reply.

If someone asks you today, "How are you?"
give a MINDFUL response.

Change it up from the typical,
"Fine" or "good, how are you?"

Actually take a second and think about it, and
respond honestly. If you're pissed off, after you've
reflected for a moment to see how you actually
ARE in that moment, then say, "I'm pissed off."

If you're pumped, say so.
If you're neutral, say so.

Prioritize giving an honest response over caring
how the person hears you.

What needs to be different in your life in order to feel completely successful? There's only one thing. And it ain't in the outer world.

The one thing is your thinking. No one is successful until they think themselves so.

Start with success mindset, don't wait for it.

Time for a fundamentals reminder: throughout the day today, ask yourself, what's my mood right now? And, if it's low grade, elevate it by strengthening your thoughts.

Here's a little nugget from my Oneness University experience in India: "Whatever you accept completely will take you to peace. Including the acceptance that you cannot accept."

Acceptance is FUNDAMENTAL to Mental Toughness and it is often completely misinterpreted as complacency or resignation. It is the opposite of that. It is powerful.

Acceptance is the often remarkably difficult and mindful CHOICE to stop struggling against what is, and to rather open up to the possibility of discovering a way to work masterfully WITH it. That approach is far superior to resignation.

## THE TRUTH:
It can't get better than this very moment.

## THE LIE:
I need something I don't have (more money, a better job, a spouse) to be infinitely happy.

## THE PRACTICE:
Catch yourself entertaining the lie and replace it with the truth.

## QUESTION:
Why *do* anything, then, if it can't get any better? Why not just sit on my ass and let it all unfold?

## ANSWER:
'Cause creating miracles is much more fun.

If you ask a golfer after his round (I'm using a male example here because it's truer in my experience for men than women in this example), "How'd it go?" the chances are very good that, unless he had an unusually good scoring round, he'll say something negative.

But if that same dude is a surfer, and you ask him after even just a very mediocre day of surfing, "How was it?" he's most likely to say someting like, "It was fun." (and after a great day of surfing, he'll say something more like, "EPIC!") Same guy.

Different surroundings/culture - different perspective. Pay attention today to the chameleon in you. Choose the inspired one more.

There is no slot for "retirement" when you're living an ALL IN! life.

Sometimes when someone is telling you a story you'vealready heard or when they're teaching you a lesson you've already had before, there's great value in replacing the thought, "I've already heard this" with "what else can I learn from this?" or "How good am I at applying this?"

**RE-MIND-ER Alert!** Take a moment right now to acknowledge deeply just two things for which you are incredibly grateful. Make this a habit. When in gratitude, it is impossible to be suffering.

Was this week or last week a crazy week? Yeah? Crazy, huh? You have "crazy weeks" in your life, do ya? (This is a setup, by the way.)

Without me needing to know one thing about your week, I can already tell you EXACTLY why it was "crazy." And I'm not even psychic (that I know of). Here it is: crazy thinking. There's no such thing as a crazy week. Or a crazy day. Or a crazy second. There's only crazy interpretations.

One of THE most intelligent, productive, lucrative and joy filled adjustments I have ever made was putting BUFFERS between ALL of my appointments - both professional and personal appointments. Creating space around them, especially when I really believed that it wouldn't be possible, changed my life profoundly.

I am exponentially more punctual (always now), present, energized, relaxed, attentive, enthused and skillful.

If you live with appointments smushed up against each other, you are struggling unnecessarily.

Treat yourself to space.

One of the reasons I love golf so much is because of the endless life lessons it teaches me. Here's one. Generally speaking, it's more important to be decisive than it is to be right.

So often we paralyze ourselves with indecision. Most usually because we have learned to fear being wrong. And in avoiding being wrong, we are delaying the opportunity to grow.

And, I'm also putting time between me and being amazing. When I make mistakes, I want to make them with confidence! And then grow from them.

There's a great shift that occurs when I change my story from "things happen TO me" to "things happen FOR me." Only when I choose to live in the latter, am I open to creating amazing outcomes from EVERYTHING!

Challenge for you for today...see how many times today you can choose ENTHUSIASTIC responses. To absolutely everything. What a miracle it would be if you could go the entire day with only those. See how close you can get. We don't need to explain why.

A favorite distinction of mine is abundance vs scarcity. I've found that the most Mentally Tough people choose to operate from an abundant mindset - meaning, they operate from the belief that there is more than enough of what we want and need AND that we each possess the resourcefulness to create what we want and need.

That belief system (choice) is empowering and it activates all forms of intelligence.

So is it right or wrong?
Who gives a shit?
If it has us create excellence, we dig it!

After college, before I embarked on my Mental Toughness Training journey, I studied Astrophysics for a semester. Learned a lot of amazing stuff from that experience.

Perhaps the most amazing takeaway is this: everything in this universe has been unfolding with flawless choreography for about 15 billion years (at the time of this writing ;))

So when you let that sink in, it's pretty comforting. And it has me feel a little silly for complaining about the traffic.

Here's a great practice for taming defensiveness (which totally deactivates intelligence). Assume everyone is in support of you.

So, for example, say someone at work today makes a snide remark to you (or at least you THINK it's a snide remark), choose to assume they are entirely well-intended. Even if you're wrong.

Just experiment with that.

Challenge for the day:
ONLY SPEAK TO YOURSELF THE WAY YOUR
COACH SPEAKS TO YOU.

If you don't have a coach, your challenge for the
day is to hire a coach. Then do the other challenge
tomorrow.

Joking aside, having a coach is a pretty smart
move. And so is being remarkably conscious of
the quality of your inner dialog.

I saw a quote recently that reads, "If you can't beat fear, do it scared." I simultaneously love and hate that quote. I don't really hate it, but the part I don't like is the implication that there would ever be a reason that someone was unable to control ther own emotions. I think that's total bullshit.

BUT, I do acknowledge that to be masterful at doing that, it DOES take practice, and most of us haven't been taught the practices (that I have committed my life to teaching).

SO, the part I love about it is, until you learn to master your states, don't let a shitty state like fear have you believe you can't still forge onward!!!

**Today's challenge: refrain from ridicule.**

**It doesn't make you stronger in any way,
and, in fact, it weakens you.
So see if you can go the day without any of it.**

**This one ain't easy.**

I'm going to share with you a phrase that I hear often in my coaching with new clients that haven't had a lot of high level coaching before.

It's pretty weak. And pretty popular. Here it is:

"That's just how I am."

Can you see why that's so weak? I love working with this thinking because it's a bonafide breeding ground for quantum growth. When you get why that's so weak, your life expands exponentially.

I had a cool interaction with my tennis coach, Suk, in my lesson this morning. She knows I'm in an aggressive physical transformation right now and conditioning is a priority, so she used that.

The entire lesson was non-stop movement. Even picking up the balls was a cardio exercise. She was yelling at me. It was awesome. Until it became annoying as fuck. And you know why it became annoying? Because I let my thinking get weak.

So I talked to her for a second. I told her I need a second to get my head right again.

I told her how brilliant this lesson was and that I am recommitting to looking at everything she has me do as fuel that's propelling me to my goal.

Then I puked.

We so often struggle so much with the actions of others, which are completely out of our control.

So something I learned from Don Miguel Ruiz in his amazing book, The Mastery of Love (he's the same dude that wrote The Four Agreements), that has been THE MOST helpful nugget with respect to not taking shit personally is this:

*"Everyone is doing the best they can with what they have available to them at the time. AND, no one really wants to hurt anyone else. The only reason we do is because of our own unhealed hurt."*

Good stuff right there.

With my private coaching clients, we are always working on killer projects. And we use timelines. And other metrics, as well, to create urgency. Why? Simple. To create more stress. Kidding. In fact, it's just the opposite. It's for FUN!!!

The rewarding fun of getting cool shit done - not because we NEED to but rather because we GET to. I'm constantly contradicting myself with these poor folks! First I tell them that none of this needs to get done and then I scold them for not getting their shit done! (It's a great gig, this coaching thing. I highly recommend it.)

The truth is, the paradox is spectacular. It doesn't NEED to get done. None of it. But the game of creating a magnificent goal, upgrading it into a decision and then making it your reality - it's miraculous. And it's what we're designed for.

## DISTINCTION FOR THE DAY:
### Incremental Growth vs Quantum Growth.

## INQUIRY FOR THE DAY:
### Am I holding myself back by expecting gradual/incremental progress when I could perhaps create a QUANTUM leap in progress?

Open that inquiry up into ALL areas of your life. Experiment with that.

And, as always, please report back to me the miracles you create as a result.

Thank you very much. ;)

Einstein said that there are only two ways to look at life. One is as if nothing is a miracle, and the other is as if everything is.

So the next time someone responds to you by saying, "Be realistic" you can reply, "I am realistic. I expect miracles."

One of my favorite mantras is, "If it ain't light, it ain't right." (it's not necessarily a beer thing.)

In Egyptian mythology there's a story that once you die, your heart is weighed against the weight of a feather. If your heart is lighter than the feather, you are free to go on and experience all the magic of the universe.

If, however, your heart is heavier than the feather, you are sent back to live again until you learn to lighten up!

Choose more lightness of being today.

The late Indian philosopher, speaker and author Jiddu Krishnamurti was once asked how he was able to remain so deeply peaceful (which is interesting because he spoke out unapologetically about how twisted society is) and he replied, "Do you want to know what my secret is? You see, I don't mind what happens."

That's not complacency. That's a masterful decision to work WITH reality.

That's some mental toughness right there.

Deliberating over whether something is possible or impossible is a waste of time.

A much more powerful way to use that time and energy would be to answer the question, "How do I most profoundly want to USE the rest of my life?"

And then to go take immediate, bold action in the direction of that.

I should really stop using "I should coments."
So should you.

Albert Ellis, possibly the meanest Psychotherapist EVER, used to scream at his clients if he heard them use an "I should" statement. He'd yell, "Stop 'SHOULDING' on yourself!"

I love that. It was his way of inviting them to stop abusing themselves with the most toxic of all human emotions - shame.

The statement, "This is a problem" never actually has to be true. You can make the argument that there are no problems in the universe, and that the only problem is the way we look at it.

So let's take starvation as an example. Or cancer. Are they "problems"? Well, I sure think so, but I also want to think of them like a math "problem" - something that needs to be solved and has a solution. That's not to minimize the issues of starvation or cancer, but rather the opposite.

I want to keep my mind right in order to keep my creative genius active so I am more likely to contribute to the discovery of that solution/cure. Again, a paradox. This Mental Toughness world seems to be full of them.

Here's the paradox in this one: I am more likely to solve the problem when I don't have a problem with the problem.

When you choose to think your way into enthusiasm (note the language there) as your response (vs reaction) to life, you activate all forms of intelligence.

Practice being more enthused today.

An observation from a Mental Coach: the more effort you put into strengthening your mind, the less effort you have to put into having, doing, or being what you want. What, specifically, will you do today to further strengthen your mind?

When I studied at The Oneness University in India, the phrase that the teachers said that stood out most for me was, "What could ever be wrong with your truth?" Think about that for a second here. How beautiful is that? How liberating is that?

## TODAY'S MENTAL TOUGHNESS PRACTICE:

Catch yourself when you get into thinking that you'reinadequate or inferior or inappropriate or mean or fat or lazy or anything else imperfect. Then replace that thinking with the thought that you're an expression of Divine Grace (use your language there) in human form.

And if you'd like to grow in some area of your life, then go do that because it's fun.

## MENTAL TOUGHNESS DAILY DISCIPLINE:

Today, when shit doesn't go as you wanted it to go, respond with the following two remarkably intelligent inquiries.

1) What's the learning in this?

2) What can I create out of exactly this?

The best way I know of stopping dwelling on the past is to stop having a problem with it.

So many of these Daily Dose messages involve the "problem" mentality. And for good reason.

You CANNOT be a Black Belt in Mental Toughness if you are not able to redirect yourself instantly - INSTANTLY - when you are interpreting reality problematically. Hold yourself to an absurdly high standard today with respect to whining, complaining or dwelling!

Activate a zero tolerance policy of complaining or regretting today. That's a bad ass mission!

Here's one of my favorites:

*"The pessimist complains about the wind. The optimist expects it to change. The realist adjusts the sails and flies across the sea."*

So both the pessimist AND the optimist are both weak because they have a problem with reality. In fact, you could argue that the so called optimist is the weakest because they're denying the reality on top of having issue with it. At least the pessimist is being straight forward with their whining.

But the strong one is the realist - the one who not only has no problem with reality, but additionally responds to it by leveraging the "problem" for something useful. THAT is mental toughness.

Today, be the realist.

Don't take your thoughts too seriously. That's where ALL of our suffering initiates - from low grade thinking (very low grade). Thoughts are nothing more than that. Just thoughts. That's it.

So catch yourself today when you're feeling unpleasant, remember that it's only because you're entertaining an unpleasant thought in that moment, and laugh at it. Laugh at the thought.

Toss it. Throw it the hell away. And replace it with one that has you remember how fucking amazing you are. That's a solid practice. Get into that.

Remember this ALL DAY today:

Life isn't happening TO you.
It's happening FOR you!

If you need to make a note
or a phone reminder to help you remember that,
DO IT!

Can you pledge to remember that
ALL DAY today?!

You know what makes it soooooo much easier to be mentally fit? Being physically fit. If you're feeling unfit, do yourself the favor of moving a little more today. Just move more than usual.

This is such a great Mental Toughness rule of thumb. Whenever you are feeling even remotely unpleasant, it is simply because in that moment you are believing a lie (a thought that is not true).

For example, you're feeling anxious because you have a shitload of work to get done in a small amount of time. Well, you aren't anxious because of that. You're anxious because you're believing the thought that if you don't get it done, you'll be screwed. THAT is the lie. And if you wanted to, you could make a very convincing argument for why you'd be screwed, but when you're really honest, you realize that argument is total bullshit.

So the three step practice here is simple: Negate the lie. Affirm the truth. Create miracles.

I want circumstances
to influence my decisions,
but not my states.

I want to respond purposefully
to what is going on in order to
maximize the probability of
being, doing or getting what I want.

But I am only able to do that when
I am in control of my emotional states.

Stay conscious of your emotions today.

Keep your states elevated.

This is more of an invitation
than a challenge or a reminder.

I invite you to take a few moments today to
redefine what the word "success" means TO YOU!

Create your own personalized definition of
success. Then take some action (no matter how
small) to further close the gap between how your
life is right now and how you defined that word.

**Reminder message today:**

**The chemicals we release in the brain from shame are the toxins. The chemicals we release from joy, gratitude, serenity, appreciation, enthusiasm, competence and love - those are the nutrients.**

**Nourish well today, my dear friend!**

One of the most neurotic cliches is this:

*"There's a time for work
and there's a time for play."*

That's horseshit.

If you look at any human peak performance research you'll rapidly discover that we are at our best when we are experiencing intrinsic reward and at play. So let's rewrite that one now.

Here's the new version:

*"I'm only interested in creating miracles,
so there's no time for work. Just play."*

One of the easiest ways for me to heighten my awareness to the quality of my thinking (which is absolutely fundamental to Mental Toughness Training) is to watch my mouth. In other words, pay close attention to the what you say out loud and be asking yourself, "Do I agree with that?"

**Mantra Alert!**

One of the best ever:

"The outer world is a reflection of the inner world."

So whatever I have going on in my life,
it's the direct reflection of what I've got
going on in my mind. Own that.

Physics has demonstrated that we live in a universe that is characterized by uncertainty.

So we have two options:

1) Struggle against that.
2) Love that.

Today, pay particular attention to when uncertainty arises in you or in your day, and check to see if you're hating or loving.

People who are ALL IN! on creating excellence in their lives always invest in themselves. They invest in their own development. Constantly.

## GET MORE SLEEP!!!

Unless you're already sleeping more than 8.5 hours a night. In which case, get your lazy ass out da bed! Most of us are not getting enough sleep.

All research shows that 8-9 hours per night is optimal for all functioning, physical and mental. Sleep deprived people are 500% more likely to have shitty thinking patterns that lead to depression.

Cognitive functioning drops drastically if you're getting less than 8 hours a night. The most Mentally Tough/most successful/happiest people in the world understand the critical function of optimal rest and schedule their lives around that.

No excuses. Except having newborns. In that case, nevermind and good luck. :)

What results are we looking for? Miracles.

What's a key component in creating miraculous results? Brain chemicals including dopamine and serotonin. What's a GREAT way to activate the release of said neurotransmitters? High grade emotional states (enthusiasm, gratitude, competence, joy, eg.).

And, finally, how do we create these high grade states? High grade THINKING!

It always comes back to being a frickin' Thought Warrior, doesn't it?! Yep.

So, today's reminder:

Only permit yourself to entertain thoughts that make you feel pumped! Catch yourself when you're feeling uncool, and immediately upgrade your thought content! DO IT!!!

I had a beautiful coaching call this morning with a client who came up with this spectacular new mantra: "I co-create magic with life. It's all I ever have time for."

How great is that?!

Co-creating magic with life. See, the magic is always there waiting for you to activate it.

In every moment there is the potential for magic to be released from it. If you'll slow down enough today, you'll notice that much more. Give it a whirl.

And as always, let me know what happened!

I'm constantly watching my mouth. What I mean is, I'm always listening to what comes out of it.

If you'll start paying closer attention to the stuff that comes out of your mouth, and listen to those words like an outsider would, you may be astonished with how much of what you say YOU think is bullshit! It's hilarious!

Observing your own language is an amazingly effective way to strengthen your mind. You listen to yourself first. Then you ask yourself, "Do I agree with what I just said?" If the answer is "no" then you modify it.

Even when giving a public talk in front of a ton of people, I'm often saying, "Delete what I just said. I don't agree with it." And people love that shit.

So I've started a new thing with all of my private coaching sessions. We're now initiating each one by sincerely answering the question, "What's legitimately AMAZING in your life right now?"

The reason I'm doing this is to get the brain primed to create miracles in the ensuing coaching session. See, when we selectively attend to that which is effortlessly inspiring and undeniably kick ass, we release those fucking gorgeous little serotonin and dopamine neurotransmitters that activate all forms of creative genius. Mmmhmmm.

It ain't about "happy thoughts." That's stupid. It's about being absurdly awesome. That's not stupid.

So, why don't you take a moment right now and just go ahead and answer that question.

What's truly AMAZING in your life right now?

**Stop complaining. It doesn't suit you.**

## Daily challenge!!!

Pay very very close attention today to the times when you are prioritizing being liked over being honest. Notice when you're avoiding the possibility of offending someone (which is actually impossible, by the way) or hurting their feelings (also impossible) by swallowing your truth.

And if you're feeling particularly courageous, then go ahead and speak your truth.

And deal masterfully with the consequences, unless the consequences are amazing. In which case celebrate that.

Overriding the learned belief that there is value in being a pleaser takes great Mental Toughness.

This is a particularly sophisticated challenge because your ego will sense when you're about to override and it'll try to fool you into thinking bullshit like, "There's no need to be so mean! Don't say that!" Your truth is divine. Trust it.

Victims of circumstance permit what's happening on the outside to govern what's happening on the inside. Weak.

Creators permit their internal states to influence what's going on in the outer world. Bad ass.

My EnterTrainer, Billy Woodmansee (follow him on social media), gave me this incredibly fun, hard pool workout yesterday.

He had me wear a sweatshirt in the pool which made it so much more challenging. At one point he had me jump out of the pool and do pushups on the pool deck. I could do TWO!!! TWO!!! Then I was toast. I actually started laughing. But then I said to myself, "YES!" And "GOOD!" And I got one more outta me. That kind of failure is so wonderful. THAT is the kind of failure I want to experience all the time when I'm pushing myself - in any context. THAT is when we grow.

So today, if you reach a point where you feel toast, remember two things: You got more in the tank (say YES and GOOD to yourself a lot), and that it is in those moments that you're getting stronger.

**Stress is a form of self-torture.
It's 100% self-inflicted. Stop it.**

The sentence, "I want happiness" is weak. Can you see why? Think about it. That's your exercise for today. I'll elaborate in tomorrow's Daily Dose.

OK, so the reason that the sentence, "I want happiness" is weak is because it arises from the belief that happiness could ever elude you.

The Emotional Master would never say this sentence. They would say something like, "I am creating happiness now."

Happiness doesn't happen TO you, you create it with high grade thinking. So the "I want" part is putting it off into the future, like a victim, awaiting some desireable event to occur before letting yourself experience joy. Not prudent.

Remember the mantra:
Create the State; Don't Wait.

Daily challenge: Challenge the notion of "impossibility." After all, that's all it is - a notion. We are in no position to act like authorities on what is possible or impossible. We use 11% of our brains. Who the hell are WE to get involved with that kind of estimation?!

So when you start to consider the improbability of something you'd like to have, be, do or create, challenge your assumptions and come at it from a place of assuming instead that it IS entirely possible and get into figuring out how.

What do Mental Toughness and service have in common? Mentally Tough people understand that there is no such thing as success if it doesn't involve, on some level, service to others.

You know when a person becomes an expert at something? It ain't the Malcolm Gladwell thing about 10,000 repetitions. Yeah, mastery must be achieved. Duh.

But I've met a lot of folks with incredible mastery who don't THINK they're experts. So the reps are there. The skill has been developed. But the expertise ain't. So until you CHOOSE to BE an expert, you are not.

And to throw a little twist into it, you can make that choice LONG before you've finished accumulating the reps. Hmmm.

One of the most powerful (and challenging) exercises that I do in my workshops and coaching sessions is entitled, The Problem is the Gift.

It involves converting situations or circumstances that you historically interpreted as problematic into actual blessings.

The challenge comes from the fact that we have become so accustomed to seeing things like traffic, for example, as a complete pain in the ass, that even beginning to entertain the notion that it isn't feels immediately hokey and insincere.

But that's simply a reflection of how deeply brainwashed we are into experiencing the miracles of life (more specifically here, the miracles of automobiles and roadways) as problems.

And when we see it from that (clear and intelligent) perspective, we can realize how stupid we're being when we complain.

So today, practice turning your "problems" around into gifts.

Here's an interesting observation:
When I'm fascinated, I can't be frustrated.

Today, choose to be fascinated by that which you
may have otherwise found frustrating.

**Remember this today:**

**You're really far better than you think you are.
But that only applies to everything.**

"The Zone" has never been described as an experience characterized by struggle. Isn't that interesting? In fact, it's almost always described as light and effortless. Experiment with that today.

You know what's an amazingly effective cure for fear? Enthusiasm. It's like shining a flashlight onto a shadow. The lightness makes the darkness disappear. Choose more (MUCH MORE) enthusiasm today, please.

I'm convinced that solutions to all of our "problems" abound.

---

*For an amazing true story on this, check out the video I recorded about my wild round trip to give a talk in San Fran one day:*
*http://bit.ly/sanfran-enthusiasm*

---

So the solutions are always there. But our doubt acts as a cloaking device to those solutions.

So today, practice reminding yourself that there IS an answer, albeit illusive perhaps. It's there. Mental Toughness is characterized by the willingnesss to KNOW without proof.

I'm always talking about using high grade thinking to create high grade states. But here's an interesting question for you today:

*"What's the state that exists in the absence of thought?"*

When I ask my clients this question, the most popular response is peace. Isn't that interesting?

So if peace or serenity simply exists without us having to create it, then how is it that we ever experience anything other than peace or serenity? We interrupt it with low grade thinking.

Peace is our default position.

I find it so interesting that when athletes are in The Zone, competitiveness isn't the top priority. Mastery is. What can you learn from that today?

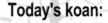

**Today's koan:**

**The less of a problem I have with the problem, the more likely I am to solve the problem.**

Worry is simply the result of imagining a disastrous future. That's true if it's two seconds or two years ahead that you're imagining. And imagining disaster creates disaster.

So if you're going to look forward, you might as well imagine perfection.

Visualize perfect outcomes today.

The biggest distinction between physical and mental training is that mental training is entirely an invisible workout. What you're strengthening can't be seen. It can only be felt.

So Mental Toughness is predicated upon awareness. We must become acutely aware of our moods in order to manipulate them at will masterfully. Practice more mood awareness today.

Former NFL star and current NFL Broadcaster, Adam Archuleta is also a former client of mine and a current friend. We have breakfast every so often.

Recently he said to me, "When I set a goal that is theoretically impossible, that's when I do my best work." The operative word in that sentence is "theoretically."

Mental Toughness is characterized by the willingness to set your targets "theoretically" out of reach and then to go do what it takes to discover that they were within reach after all.

"That's so irritating" is a phrase that is NEVER true. It seems true when we are being victim thinkers. But it is still never true.

Nothing can irritate you. You only feel irritated when you interpret something problematically. Own that and you're free.

Today, practice upgrading interpretations of stuff you historically interpreted as irritating.

Here's a real practical Mental Toughness nugget for ya: The Post-Game Routine.

After a performance of any kind ( a game, a negotiation, a recital, a presentation) has just ended, answer the following three questions in this order:

1) How was I AMAZING?
2) What's the one BIG lesson in this for me?
3) What, specifically, will I do to grow from it?

Do you have a Success Story file?

It's a place where you save all of your greatness stories. If you don't, start one. Add to it every time you have a big win or get a great piece of feedback.

Then, access it frequently. It is a great tool to help you create the state of competence and expertise.

A definition of anxiety is the unpleasant, and toxic, emotion that arises solely from thinking about the future in a disasterous way. It's the product of thinking about what COULD go wrong at some point in the near or distant future.Anxiety cannot exist when I'm fully present with this moment.

So today, please treat yourself well and remember to use your ability to catch yourself when you are worrying about anything off in the future and bring your awareness back to this moment by instead choosing to think about a few things for which you are truly grateful.

Waiting is the enemy of excellence.

We've been conditioned to wait for so many things - unnecessarily. We wait until we have a certain number of zeroes in our bank account before we feel wealthy, or even safe. We wait until we have a certain title before we feel successful. We wait for recognition before we feel competent.

Feelings of wealth, success and competence are emotions. And we create our emotions with our thoughts. So this is your reMINDer to choose to BE wealthy, successful and competent, and everything else you want to feel, today by thinking that way.

Remember the mantra:
"Create the state - don't wait!"

I am more likely to solve the "problem" when I don't have a problem with the problem. In fact, I can do even better than that.

If I am willing to explore how the "problem" could actually be a gift or a blessing, then I'm really activating creative genius and now I can make a miracle out of it.

You have the ability to choose that you will create your desires without first knowing the how. The "how" is in the "what" and you activate those mechanics by taking immediate action.

Today's invitation: play with the power of positively acknowledging someone for who and how they are. Tell them what you dig about them. It's free nourishment for the soul. For both of you.

We have a lot of stupid sayings that I'd like to make sure we aren't buying into. Today's target is, "Thank God it's Friday! (T.G.I.F.)"

It's become so popular that there's even a successful restaurant chain named after it! So the complete sentence would be, "Thank God it's finally the weekend so I can finally let myself feel joy since the hell of my shit job is over for a couple days!"

If you're thinking this way, PLEEEEEASE hire a coach and have them help you restructure your life so you can greet each and every day with,"Thank God it's TODAY!"

When I was a high school and college athlete, I was good. I wasn't great. At least not consistently. And the reason why is that I waited until I screwed up and got pissed before I got determined and focused. But by then, it was often too late in the game to make a difference, or I'd get benched by the coach. I really believed that my anger fueled me. And it did a little.

But think about how much time and opportunity I wasted by waiting for my anger. I didn't know then that I could've bypassed the mistakes and the anger and could've chosen determination nand focuse in my warm-ups.

How might this apply to you in your life?

**Reminder:**

**The better you FEEL, the better you ARE. At everything. (Except being lame.)**

**Elevate your state often today!**

The pessimist complains about the wind. The optimist is sure it'll go away. Meanwhile, the realist sets their sails and flies across the sea. All circumstances are leveragable.

Find the gifts today. Be a realist. Be in alignment with reality. Work with it. Leverage on!

Let's have today be a "Get To" day vs. a "have to" day. When you're in the "Get To" mentality, you're activating enthusiasm which in turn activates badassery.

I love the word "inspiration."

It means being in alignment with your spirit. And a real key here is to not WAIT for something or someone to inspire you. Again, the mantra, "Create the state - don't wait."

Talk to yourself right now in a way that you'd talk to a loved one if you were trying to inspire them.

Inspire yourself!

Activate spirit!

Be that person today. Watch how your vibe interfaces with the world. It's nice.

Let's consider the term, "inconvenient." It's nothing more than a judgment call to deem something inconvenient, isn't it?

So the question becomes, "Does that interpretation serve me? Does it have me be smart? Does it have me be powerful?"

We know the answer.

So today, choose to have nothing be inconvenient. Instead experiment with it being opportune. That takes some real work to do that.

That's an actual exercise I use with myself daily and with my coaching clients. It's powerful as hell.

Have fun with that!

Mental Toughness is completely predicated by self-inquiry. Inward awareness. Pay close attention today to your emotions and your language. Both are clear reflections of your thinking, and we're all interested here in becoming Thought Warriors.

Pain is inevitable; suffering is optional.

The difference is that I suffer when I judge the pain as a problem. If I'd just permit myself to fully experience the pain (sadness, for example), instead of wishing it was gone, it can actually be a sweet experience. And I won't suffer.

"The struggle is real!" Unless it isn't.

"This sucks!" Unless it doesn't.

Always your call. Choose wisely today.

I am convinced that magic is available to us in each moment. That's the constant. The variable is our willingnesss to slow down enough and vibe high enough to co-create with it.

In Mental Toughness context, surrender is an extremely disciplined practice. It requires tremendous psychological mastery, which comes from the practice of perpetually examining and upgrading the activity of your mind.

Surrendering is knowing when the best choice of action in a given moment is actually non-action.

It's nothing like the "I give up!" definition of surrender. Unless you're giving up trying to force shit. Those are the exact circumstances when surrender is the masterful choice.

Practice no forcing today. In other words, practice the mastery of mindful surrender, or working WITH the forces that be.

Since the Big Bang, everything - EVERYTHING - has been unfolding with flawless choreography.

From the ratio of particles to anti-particles in the milliseconds after that kaboom, to the ratio of hydrogen and helium in stars to permit supernova - the most cataclysmic event in the universe - from which the building blocks of life arise (carbon, for example). To the mass and distance of our moon that permits our livable atmosphere. All flawless. Precise. In inconceivable ways.

Incorporate this mantra into your life:

*"Everything is unfolding exactly as it should."*

That one mantra has changed my life profoundly.

In research with centenarians (people 100 years old or more, in case you aren't familiar), when asked the question, "Looking back, what would you do differently?" there is some really interestying uniformity in responses.

Three of the most popular were these:

1) I'd take more risks.

2) I'd slow down and appreciate how beautiful life is all by itself without me having to do anything.

3) I'd be way less obsessed with my own success and far more concerned with making a difference and leaving a legacy.

There's such great wisdom in this advice.
Stay present with these today.

I was at an amazing conference in Sardinia, Italy recently and the theme was Longevity - what has people live long and healthy lives (Sardinia is a "blue zone" where people live really long).

One of the things I learned there that stunned me is this: loneliness is more toxic than morbid obesity AND smoking! That blew my mind.

Now, one of the greatest books I've ever read is entitled, Love, Freedom, Aloneness by Osho. In it, he says, "Loneliness is the absence of the other. Aloneness is the presence of one's self." That also struck me when I read that. Deeply.

Can you see the distinction?

So by now, you've gathered that I really love and rely upon the deep power and value of mantras. And here's one of my favorites:

*"I am instantly and inextricably connected to all that exists across spacetime."*

Quantum physics shows us that, at the most fundamental level, everything is energy and information AND that energy and information do not travel. They are instantaneously accessible regardless of distance. ANY distance. Which means everything is connected. That's pretty comforting. If I can remember that.

I have a new mantra:

*"Find the Magic in the mundane."*

It's the result of a phenomenal coaching session I had today with one of my clients. (Hi, Terry!) The meaning behind it is simple.

Magic is happening all around us at all times. That's the constant in the equation. The variable is US - our willingnesss or ability to slow DOWN enough and vibe HIGH enough so that we can participate with and co-create with the magic.

Think about a trip you had, a holiday or some fantastic amazing journey when you felt awe-inspired. Do that now. And then take that emotion and carry it with you ALL DAY today!!

And watch the magic unfold. No joke!

I was in a coaching session yesterday with my loooong time client, Alex Bennett. Alex and I have been coaching together for 10 years so we have achieved very high context communication.

That's like when you know exactly what the other person is about to say before they say it and they know what your response is before you say it.

So we were working on a very important Mental Toughness Tool that needs regular drilling. The skill is being able to respond perpetually to the question, "What's AMAZING?"

After he went on for a while with his responses, he said, "I have goosebumps." And we decided that it's a good idea to "Live in Goosebumps!"

So that's our new mantra and he's given you permission to use it! ;)

I attended a remarkable event in Sardinia, Italy last month and the theme of it was Longevity. One of the variables that contributes significantly to living a long and healthy life is community.

Feeling connected and included is so powerful. The 300 or so fellow attendees at this conference/party had what I now refer to as the "Tribe Vibe" and the founder of the event informed us in his opening keynote that although the majority of us had never met each other, by virtue of being there together for this common intertest, we were all already friends. And I just found that to be remarkably heartwarming.

I'm practicing applying that notion, that we're all members of the same Tribe, the human Tribe, wherever I go now. (I'll have a follow up on this one tomorrow...stay tuned.)

So following up on the "Tribe Vibe" here's an invitation for you to play around with.

As you go into any interaction with other people today and the next several days, beforehand, open your heart. And I mean that.

Open your heart up and start with love. In other words, don't wait (remember, the enemy of excellence is waiting) to see how the other/s is/are being before you vibe high.

Initiate the interaction with high vibes, love, compassion, openness, connectedness - without having to say even a single word - and be the forerunner. The initiator.

Let your high grade energy be a silent invitation for the rest to join.

Time to rip on another stupid saying.

*"Good things come to those who wait."*

So, if that was meant to mean, "Don't force shit" then that's what the saying should be. But I suspect it wasn't originally used in that context.

Now, I'm a huge fan of trusting timing, and I see that as a true art form. But as you may have gathered, I am NOT a fan of waiting unnecessarily. And there's a whole lot of unnecessary waiting going on in the world.

So, our new version of that phrase is:

*"Miracles are co-created by those who Decide, get ALL IN! and take immediate, bold and masterful action."*

We're gonna need to shorten that, but it's a start.

When I hear a client say to me in a coaching session, "I'm overwhelmed!" I know in that moment that I really need to serve them immediately by lovingly and unapologetically calling them out on their victim thinking.

Being "overwhelmed" is a "happening to me" interpretation of reality. It's weak and never true. It deactivates intelligence.

The powerful interpretation of reality is the "happening FOR me" approach where I act like the creator of my life and discover ways to work WITH what's happening to create greatness.

**Mantra suggestion for the day:**

*"Ain't bad; just is."*

**Sakespeare said, "Nothing is good or bad until we think it so." And he's right!**

So practice having your lowest interpretation of events today be neutral. Just is. At worst.

Presidential Pardons are rather fascinating to me. So just before the President leaves office, they get to pardon people for anything without having to give any justification for it whatsoever. None. They're just pardoned. Simple as that.

So what if we had that same privelege of pardoning, but pardoning OURSELVES - without having to supply ANY justification whatsoever - for anything and everything that we've ever felt guilty about? Hmmmm.

**Start today with this question:**
**"How can I serve today?"**

Osho is one of my favorite authors/teachers. One of my favorite sayings of his is:

*"Lonliness is the absense of the other. Aloneness is the presence of one's self."*

So, not feeling loved is simply you not loving yourself. Where's the Mental Toughness in that?!

When I was studying in India,
I asked one of the teachers there what her
definition of enlightenment was?

She smiled hugely and then stared at the ceiling,
still smiling, for about 30 seconds and then looked
back at me joyfully and said, "Having no internal
conflict." Choose peace today. A lot.

You know what's a great sign of a Mentally Tough Bad Ass? Being loveable.

So who is loveable? Someone who craves love? Yeah, no. Or is it the one who is at ease with themselves? Be loveable today.

Feels like a good time to do a "Success" check up. So, IF we agree just for today, to define success as having your life on your terms, how successful are you? What would you need to change in order to be a bit more successful today or in the very near future?

Mental fitness and physical fitness are inextricably interwoven. How's your level of physical fitness these days? If you are happy with it, celebrate that right now. If you are dissatisfied with your fitness level, what commitment are you willing to make RIGHT NOW to change that?

Today's Mental Toughness exercise is to examine your beliefs about money. Do your thoughts about money have you feel anxious and urgent? Do your thoughts around money have you feel playful and excited? If they aren't the latter, re-author your money stories.

I'm taking tennis lessons. And my coach, Suk (pronounced sook), who is from Malaysia, is always getting deep on me - which I love.

She talks about being in meditative states like when you're bouncing the ball pre-serve, and she also talks a lot about how effortless perfect shots feel when executed with proper form.

So I'm going to go ahead and start calling this "Radical Effortlessness."

She pushes me and pushes me really hard and creates ways for me to work my ass off so that I can earn the effortlessness.

When I hit a pure shot with that perfect form, she stops and just smiles and that's my cue to notice the effortlessness. And it sinks in deeper so it becomes easier to access. Isn't that cool?

Slow down today and notice your mastery - your Radical Effortlessness that you've earned.

An "aha!" moment is a very powerful transformative moment.

I give my coaching clients lots of fun puzzles and riddles and such to stimulate creativity and expansive thinking.

When they either arrive at the solution, or when they see me give the solution, they have an "Aha" experience and I ask them to sit still quietly in that moment (I actually advise them in advance to prepare for the aha) and get familiar with it.

It's the experience of the mind expanding back into creative genius - the way it was before we were educated about our limitations.

It's an experience of remembering and it's powerful. Notice your aha's today and let the experience sink in.

We live in a universe that is characterized by uncertainty. Fact. I'm certain of it. :)  So, our options are, (a) hate that, or (b) love that. We know the Mentally Tough choice. Embrace Uncertainty today, my Mentally Tough comrade!!!

When you argue with someone, who is arguing? It's actually not you. It's your beliefs. Your beliefs are arguing with the beliefs of the other. Isn't that interesting? So today, have a fun look at your beliefs about arguing.

If you think of your negativity as "garbage", then someone is always collecting your garbage. We are always either polluting or purifying the world with our thinking. Purify more today.

Here's a great Mental Toughness Tool for ya today. I call it, "Virtual Do-overs."

After any event has ended that you don't feel you handled well or performed well in, you get to do several imaginary do-overs in your mind's eye and let those rewire your neural patterns.

Imagine yourself reliving the experience but being completely masterful. Imagine pure perfection. And know that those images are literally making you better.

Here's a good, tough challenge for today.
We'll call it "Relaxed Responding."

So say someone tells you today that you look
really angry. Your mind will potentially want to
react to that with defensiveness. "Why do you say
that?" "What do you mean?"

The mind is always so ready to react, to explain,
to defend, to form a conclusion.

See if you can just let the mind relax today so the
response would be more like, "I see."

All fear exists in anticipation, not in reality.

So, today, be an Emotional Warrior and be willing to be wrong. And be amazing at it.

Be amazingly wrong.

The #1 mistake people make
in the pursuit of excellence?

Waiting.

We wait for good results before we let ourselves
experience the internal states that render
greatness. Create the state – don't wait.

Before you engage in any important event or
performance, take a few moments and
intentionally put yourself into a super solid state
of mind. Get fired up. Get relaxed. Get focused.
Get certain. Get into your expert self.

Choose to get great – before your gig even starts.
It's what the greats do.

Create the state. Don't wait.

A client of mine recently sent me the book, You are a BADASS, by Jen Sincero (thank you, Vickie!).

My favorite sentence thus far, and I doubt she's gonna top this one, is this:

*"There's nothing more unstoppable than a freight train full of fuck-yeah."*

Don't know if I could love that too much more.

So you're the freight train and when you choose to think your way into enthusiasm by pumping your mind full of amazing thoughts (try it now, it works really fast and really well), you become the badass you were designed to be.

Alan Watts is one of my favorite authors and lecturers. YouTube search him, and have a listen for a couple minutes. He's got a GREAT laugh and he uses it liberally.

Here's a quote from his book, aptly entitled, The Book. Ha! The subtitle is, On the Taboo Against Knowing Who You Are.

*"We do not 'come into' this world; we come OUT of it, as leaves from a tree. As the ocean 'waves,' the universe 'peoples'."*

We are all connected.

Shame is quite possibly
THE most toxic of all human emotions.

Rate yourself on a scale of 1-10 (where 10 is high)
on how much you shame yourself on a daily basis
with thoughts like, "I shouldn't have said that!" Or,
"I should really lose weight." "I should have my
shit together." "I should be a better
father/mother/spouse/etc."

As the meanest therapist in history (besides me -
before I shifted to coaching and got even meaner),
Albert Ellis, used to scream at his clients when
they used the "should" word, "STOP
'SHOULDING' ON YOURSELF!!!"

Shame on you for shaming yourself!

No shaming today, please.

We are always acting either
out of LOVE or out of FEAR.

It's really that simple.

So the practice is to self-inquire. Heighten your
internal awareness of your emotional states and
categorize them into one of those two categories.
That's the first step. And if you're in a fear state,
you can elevate by adjusting the way you're
thinking in that moment.

Speak to yourself differently, lovingly, confidently,
joyfully. Notice the lightness. This is a remarkably
sophisticated practice in Mental Toughness. And
it's infinitely liberating and motivating.

**Resentment is very expensive.**

**Reallocate those funds. Pick just one person for whom you are harboring some anger. Then reallocate by simply waiving it. Just waive it.**

**Gone. Poof. All done. Have a great day.**

"Realistic" is such a relative term, the definition of which ranges so drastically from person to person that it seems wholly useless.

I am far more interested in spending my mental energy on assessing DESIRE and then taking IMMEDIATE action toward that desire. And watching what happens. And loving it.

Here's a cool mantra for ya today:

*"I am superior to no one. I am inferior to no one."*

It's great because that tiny little phrase can have a huge calming effect. Give it a spin.

I'm a big time Villanova hoops fan, and a huge fan of their uber classy coach, Jay Wright.

As a child, I went to basketball camp there with his predecessor, the late Rollie Massimino. In Coach Wright's book, Attitude: Develop a Winning Mindset On and Off the Court, he points out that a vital element of being a top shelf team or organization is honoring the organization and individuals who came before you, because your success is their success too.

Take a moment today and acknowledge someone or someones who laid the foundation for you. There's great Mental Toughness in that.

A guy named Ichijirou Araya climbed Mount Fuji. (I know, that does sound like the opening of a joke, like "A Japanese guy walks into a bar..." But it isn't. It's simply a statement of fact.)

Why is it significant? Well, only because he was 100 years old at the time.

What are your beliefs about age and aging, and even dying, for that matter?

Examine them today.

Ask yourself if you agree with them.

And if you don't love them, delete them and completely rewrite them so that they SERVE you.

I used to coach a lot of pro golfers
before shifting predominantly into coaching in the
corporate world. Unsurprisingly, and very
pleasantly, Mental Toughness Training in the two
worlds is fundamentally identical.

So instead of going to all these PGA tournaments
around the US, now I get to watch them from my
armchair in the comforts of my living room.

And EVERY SINGLE TIME, I hear an announcer
say something like, "Well, he just needs to make a
few good putts to get his confidence back."

And then I cringe.

It gives me agita!
(Google that one. It's pretty funny.)

Can you get why that comment is completely
backwards???

Following up on the last Daily Dose,
the reason the notion that good results need to
occur in order to feel confident is so backwards,
is because confidence
(like EVERY other human emotional state)
is the product of your thoughts,
NOT your outcomes.

So you don't need to wait (the archenemy of all
excellence) for anything to feel confident. In fact,
the Mentally Tough approach is to START with it.

Today, actively THINK yourself into a mega-
confident state before doing anything important.

Talk to yourself like an absolute Champ.

Remember only your greatness and your
successes beforehand.

Create the state - don't wait!

I love Ben Franklin for a multitude of reasons. Among them are these quotes: "The things which hurt, instruct." And also, "Beer is proof that God loves us and wants us to be happy."

But let's address the first one. My revision of it is, "The things that hurt, CAN instruct, if we interpret them masterfully (with Mental Toughness)."

Adversity (which itself is simply an interpretation and can be questioned always) doesn't automatically teach us or bring value.

The potential for that is always there, but in order for us to grow and benefit from it, we must CHOOSE to interpret it as a real opportunity to create from. Practice that today.

Authority is such a cool word.

The root of it is the word, author.
And we are all authors.

We author the stories that we entertain all day about what's true and real. Some of those stories serve us, some don't. And as the authorities of our lives, we get to reauthor the ones that weaken us.

So your invitation for Mental Toughness Training today is this: watch your mouth.

Listen to your words; listen to what you say.

Our language is a dead giveaway to our beliefs. After you speak, ask yourself if you completely agree with what you've said, as if someone else said it.

If you don't agree, rewrite that story, Author!

Dedication is a HUGE element of Mental Toughness. Dedicating an act or a project or a performance, or even a workout, to someone outside yourself is tremendously powerful.

It creates both accountability as well as connectedness and even gratitude. And all of that strengthens you. And that's just beautiful.

Use the tool of dedication today in your activities.

Rock on!

William James, the father of modern day psychology, said,

*"The greatest weapon against stress is your ability to choose one thought over another."*

Today's Mental Training discipline is to catch yourself as many times as possible throughout the day when you're feeling any stress at all.

Then simply change the way you're thinking about the thing. Don't think of something else entirely. That's not Mental Toughness. That's avoidance.

Change the WAY you're thinking about the same thing. THAT'S one helluva drill.

In human peak performance research it's always true that the better we feel, the better we do. But only always. And in health research, it's proven that laughter is remarkably healthy.

Laughter releases the neurotransmitters in the brain that have us be awesome. But only at everything. (Except being depressed.)

So today's Mental Toughness Training invitation is to actively LOL more! Laugh. Out Loud. A lot.

And know that as you do, you're becoming healthier and more Mentally Tough.

How cool is THAT?!

When athletes talk about being "In the zone," they always describe a state of real presence.

So here's a quick, simple and powerful (great combo there) Mental Toughness Training exercise that strengthens your ability to get present instantly.

Go through the 5 senses one by one, for about 10 seconds each, and tell yourself what you're aware of.

In between each sense, go to the awareness of your thoughts. Simply pay attention to what you're thinking in that moment.

Don't manipulate the thoughts, just observe them.

Then go to the next sense.

That's a solid 2 minute Mental Workout.

Don Miguel Ruiz is such a great author. He writes on ancient Toltec wisdom. In his most famous book, The Four Agreements, he says,

*"Don't take anything personally.
Nothing others do is because of you."*

So brilliant. And in a later book, The Mastery of Love, he elaborates on that by saying,

*"No one ever really wants to hurt another.
The only reason we do is because
of our own unhealed hurt."*

Together, these two awarenesses bring enormous emotional freedom.

So today's practice is this: notice when you're taking something personally,
and recite to yourself the mantra,

*"It's not about me."*

Thomas Edison was totally Mentally Tough. Such a badass. He said,

*"When you have exhausted all possibilities, remeber this - you haven't."*

How great is that?!

Remeber that in your endeavors today.

A monk walked by a beggar sitting on the sidewalk who stopped him and asked, "Brother, do you have any food?" The monk stopped, bent down and opened up the satchel he was carrying and said, "I believe so. Let's have a look."

Together they looked inside the bag and to the astonishment of the beggar, he saw that one of the objects inside was an unusually large precious gem. The monk grabbed a sandwich and handed it to the beggar, as the beggar said, "Thank you. And, how about that beautiful gem, do you think I might have that as well."

The monk without hesitation said, "Of course." And to even greater astonishment, the beggar was handed it. Off walks the monk.

A couple days go by and they meet again. The beggar stops the monk again, reaches out and hands him back the stone. The monk asks why, and the beggar says, "I don't need it. What I need is what permitted you to so freely part with it."

The story about the monk, the beggar and the precious stone from the last Daily Dose is about one of the more challenging Mental Toughness (and Eastern Philosophical) disciplines: non-attachment. One of my favorite mantras about emotional freedom is:

*"I am open to everything and attached to nothing."*

Today's Mental Toughness Training practice is to heighten your awareness to what you think you NEED. You need food and water, and air. What else do you REALLY NEED?

I have so many wonderful different desires, but I don't want to confuse them with needs. When I get that confused, I weaken myself and I struggle and suffer.

Pay attention to what you think you really NEED today and question it.

The, "Flow State" is synonymous with the term, "The Zone." They both refer to the psychological state that we are in when we're crushing it.

And I love the term "flow" because it's what water does in a stream.

When water comes to a river rock, it doen't arrive at it, stop and say, "We have a problem here. There's an obstacle." It simply flows gracefully around it, without any hesitation, or loss of momentum. That's the effortlessness of excellence.

Be like the water today and practice flow.

Isn't it fascinating that near death experiences are always described as peaceful?

Maybe they aren't ALWAYS, but I have never heard of one that wasn't.

So assuming they are (or at least the vast majority are) serene, then let's entertain the question (because we can):

*"What if there's NOTHING to be afraid of?"*

What if it's true that EVERYTHING we fear doesn't need to be feared? Just consider that today.

Think about your greatest fears. The darkest ones. And simply open up to the possibility that not even those need to be feared.

This is a very sophisticated exercise in Mental Toughness.

And it can also be potentially life altering.

What if there's really NOTHING to be afraid of?

# VIBE UP!

That's a mantra I use with my coaching clients.
It's not just a mantra, it's a discipline.

Before you do anything important today, take a
few moments to get your vibe on.

Get enthused. Get amped. Get confident. Get
loving. Get needless. Get your vibe high.

This is science - not woo woo bullshit. Our vibes
are both measurable and detectable by each
other. You already know that. The higher the vibe,
the higher the probability of amazing outcomes.

Start with a high vibe and watch
how that affects things in your world.

Do you believe things are happening TO you or happening FOR you?

Today, please commit to testing out the notion that everything - and I mean EVERYTHING - is happening FOR you.

And feel free (as always, by simply responding to this email) to let me know what you observed.

What is you purpose?

In ONE sentence, can you answer that?

If not, think it through and craft a beautiful sentence that answers that.

That answer, that sentence, is like a North Star for you. And a powerful reason to stay committed when you feel discouraged. It's your "WHY", and when you're connected with your why, you can deal with any "how."

My purpose is this:

*"To bring lightness of being to the planet."*

I could elaborate upon that all day, but simply reciting that brief sentence to myself throughout the day empowers the hell out of me.

What is your purpose?

Do you know how easy it is to break a thinking habit? These thinking habits are so frail.

Like, "I'm a procrastinator. It's just how I am." That's absolute bullshit. It's just a weak thought.

What would the opposite of that be? What would the powerful, polar opposite of that be?

*"I get shit done. I crush. It's how I choose to show up. THAT'S who I am!"*

Today, choose ONE weak belief/thought habit and totally turn it around and recite it to yourself 200 times. New habit forming. Power up.

I had someone respond to one of these Daily Dose messages the other day (which, by the way, I highly encourage because I love hearing from The Tribe) asking,

"How do I remain positive when X is happening?"

There wasn't an X, they had a specific set of circumstances. But it doesn't matter. Because you can replace X with absolutely ANYTHING and the answer remains the same.

The way to intentionally create an elevated state - in an instant's time - is to elevate the quality of your thinking in that moment.

When you become a
Thought Warrior (with daily practice)
you automatically become an Emotional Master.

Piggy backing off the last Daily Dose, if you are genuinely interested in mastering your emotions, I cannot overemphasize the importance of committing to practicing every single day - ALL DAY - paying attention to your moods and tracing them back to your thoughts.

When you catch yourself feeling unpleasant, upgrade the way you're thinking. Right then and there. In that exact moment.

Don't change WHAT you're thinking about. Change the WAY you're thinking about it.

Accumulate thousands of repetitions of that and you will be both a Thought Warrior and an Emotional Master.

I was driving home from Whole Paycheck - I mean Whole Foods - earlier today when I drove into a moth. Or it flew in front of my car. Probably dead.

My instant auto-response was, "Aw, that sucks for the little guy." That was unpremeditated. No reflection upon that whatsoever.

So after I noticed that I said to myself, "Unless it doesn't." How do I know if that sucks for a moth?

The point here isn't about whether or not is sucks for the moth.

The point is that this is an example of the kind of meta-thinking (thinking about your thinking) that turns into Mental Toughness.

Notice your auto-responses and then ask yourself, do I agree with that?

**Here's a simple one for today's practice:**

**Be willing to be wrong.**

**There is great freedom and intelligence in that.**

I was having a conversation in the Green Room of a theater in Mumbai one time with Deepak Chopra (don't most stories start that way?).

It was moments before he was going on stage to deliver a lecture for thousands of people. He was asking me all these questions about the experience I had just had at The Oneness University in southern India.

I said to him, "Deepak, you're going on stage in like three minutes. In front of thousands of people. Do you need to collect your thoughts? Are you nervous?"

His response, "Chris, I don't do nervous. I haven't been nervous since I was 13. It didn't work for me."

So that's an option.

Diversity of experience facilitates Mental Toughness. At a conference I recently attended on Longevity I learned that having planned "Extraordinary Experiences" that are at least 250 miles away from your home is a significant variable in living a long and healthy life.

And it's not just "getting away."

These experiences are expansive and rewarding. Do you have these in your life?

*"You are infinite possibilities."*

This is one of my favorite mantras. Although I recite it to myself in the first person,

*"I am infinite possibilities."*

Notice it doesn't say I am 'capable' of infinite possibilities. It says I AM infinite possibilities. And there's a MASSIVE difference.

Fundamentally, at the quantum level, everything is energy. Which means all is connected.

So I am "capable of" separates me from all. I AM all possibilities. Let that simmer and go create miracles from that state.

**One of the best pieces of advice I ever got was this: when you wake up, replace the "I have to" with the "I get to". (And mean it.)**

This quote is from
my former coach, Steve Chandler:

*"Old patterns of thought are really the only
problem we ever have."*

And those patterns are fragile and thus can be
easily replaced with new ones that serve us.

Heighten your awareness to
your thought patterns.

Pay attention to your language.
Pay attention to your mood -
they always originate from your thoughts.

I have a relatively new mantra that I am programming my brain to use as a default response to everything. Here it is:

*"This is the best damn thing that could've happened."*

Then I ask myself AND ANSWER the question:

*"What can I create from this that I wouldn't have been able to create if not for this?"*

There are so many cool definitions of enlightenment. One of them is the ability to live blissfully detached from outcome.

How does that work? Almost sounds like complacency or apathy. But it isn't. It's at the opposite end of the power spectrum from those.

The true mental warriors in life combine two ingredients in their success recipe:

1) Absolute commitment to cause.
(ALL IN! Action)

2) Total surrender to outcome
(Infinite Acceptance) Practice that today.

Here's an elaboration on the last Daily Dose...

Be blissfully detached from outcome.

Know that you are the uncertainty that
characterizes all that is so there is
no need to worry about
whether you get what you intended or not.

What you intended isn't important when you
acknowledge that this all has been unfolding with
flawless choreography for 15 billion years!

This is a fun one. Here's a convo I had today with someone who reached out to me on LinkedIn:

THEM: Great to connect with you. I noticed your background. Do you keep your professional business options open?

ME: Not sure what you're asking, Sir.

THEM: Are you open to additional income?

ME: That's a ridiculous question, Man. No, I'm not. I have nowhere to put it. I just have nowhere else remaining to put any cash. Get straight to what you want or take your cheesy approach elsewhere.

Mental Toughness Tip of the day - you know it. DON'T BE THAT GUY!!! Start with SERVICE.

Remember the Beautiful Paradox:
*"When you prioritize service over profit is when you profit most."*

When I'm working with a coaching client who is struggling in some way, I like to ask them: "What if this was the way your life was always going to be? Precisely as it is in this moment? It'll never change. This is as good as it gets. (Great movie!) Do you think you could find a way to love it?"

This is an important line of questioning. If the answer is no, you will suffer forever as you wait for things to be different in order to choose bliss.

Mental Toughness Tip of the day: If you're sadly or disappointedly thinking that something is missing or lacking in your life, tweak that belief into this: "What could I POSSIBLY create from this?"

That's a very masterful shift from scarcity thinking to abundant thinking. From victim to creator. And that's some powerful shiz right there.

I use the terms "Mental Toughness" and "Enlightenment" synonymously.

You could say that both are defined as the ability to choose peace amidst chaos.

On defensiveness: it ain't about you!

What if you could permanently free yourself from all the effort of defending yourself? All that heavy, distracting, icky effort. Gone. And it's possible.

When we can remember that there can be nothing wrong with our truth,
then we can stop needing to defend.

Today, practice relinquishing the need to defend.

I'm gonna hook you up right now with a little lightness of being reminder. Ready?

## SNAP OUT OF IT!!!

Stop thinking all this shit "needs" to get done! NONE of it NEEDS to get dome. Really. NONE. OF. IT. You just think it does and you think it so vehemently that it OWNS you. You're a slave to it.

Snap out of that thinking and remember - right now - that all the things that you may have been losing sleep over and ruminating about throughtout the day - all the shit that's been "haunting you" - doesn't need to get done.

Now, with that in mind (or with that mindset), what still seems fun and rewarding?

You GET TO go do that.

There's magic to be had today.

Re-MIND-er for the day: slow down, vibe up and go co-create some of it!

Mental Do-Overs. Great Mental Toughness Tool.

So after you finish some type of event or performance, like a sales call, or a presentation, or a game, or even a conversation with someone, and you think it could've gone better, do mental do-overs. Re-experience the event in your mind's eye and visualize a MUCH more desirable performance.

Literally experience yourself crushing it.

Your mind-body will store that imagery as real experience. So you're more likely to act that way next time.

**Mental Toughness requires integrity.**

**Integrity is doing what you say you'll do.**
**Be impeccable with your word today.**

**Only give extremely mindful "yeses"**
**and be liberal with your "no's."**

If I'm being interviewed for a podcast or a radio show, at the end I'm often asked to give one piece of Mental Toughness advice to the listeners. I almost always go with,

*"Start stopping complaining and replace the complaints with expressions of sincere Gratitude."*

Keep a complaint journal and start to heighten your awareness to your most frequent complaints.

Pre-emptively create gratitude statements you can say to yourself as replacement thoughts and use them when you find yourself whining again.

**Today's mantra:**

*"There is no such thing as failure,
there are only results."*

AND, we love all the results. We get to celebrate
when we get the intended results. And we get to
grow when we don't. From that Mentally Tough,
highly intelligent perspective, you can't lose.

I take a lot of heat when I suggest that depression is TOTALLY treatable WITHOUT medication. And I don't give a damn.

Science backs it. Intelligent physicians do as well. Pharmaceutical companies sure don't.

And I have worked with hundreds of people closely, 1:1, who have had depression on some level. I don't recommend people on depression meds abruptly stop taking them.

But I certainly DO advise all of us to invest a lot of effort into strengthening our abilities to elevate state by strengthening the quality of our thoughts.

Then, over time, we have trained our brains to release the good chemicals that come free, and the synthetic anti-depressants become unnecessary.

I was reading some Joseph Campbell today. He's the guy who always said, "Follow your bliss."

Because when you follow your bliss and are engaged deeply in that which you love, you activate all forms of creative genius and you open doors for yourself that you didn't know were even there. Trust the organizing intelligence inherent within your passions.

Today, take a moment to write down a passion of yours that you haven't invested in lately, or ever.

Write it down. And stare at it.

Then make a decision and make a move! Any move. Just move towards it, somehow.

Activate the mechanics.
Unveil the doors.
And run through them!

One of the Mental Toughness Tools
that's integral to success (having your life on your
terms) is called Trusting Timing.

I can do everything in my power to make
something happen: I can elevate my state, I can
decide and get ALL IN!, I can take immediate
action, I can enlist the support of my
accountability team, I can dedicate my actions to
something or someone outside of me, I can use
metrics, and I can recommit often, and yet I still
must trust the rightness of natural timing.

Consider the farmer and the seeds he plants.

He doesn't plant them, water them and
then stand over them getting impatient
because they aren't sprouting immediately.

It's a beautiful balance between action and
surrender that creates excellence.

I was driving on the highway the other day when a stone smacked loudly into my windshield and created a "spider" crack in it directly in front of my face. My immediate (weak and mindless) reaction was, "Aw, Shit!"

And I immediately caught myself below the O-Line and replaced my response with this alternative story: "Thank you, windshield, for saving my FACE!" I replaced the complaint with an authentic expression of gratitude.

That's a solid Mental Toughness rep.

That's the practice.

Accumulate thousands and thousands of these reps and you are powerfully reprogramming yourself to respond to reality purposefully and with mastery.

I do puzzles every day.

There's a lot of research that supports a strong relationship between doing puzzles and brain health. And I sure love that. But one of the other reasons I love puzzles so much is that they remind me that there's always a solution.

No matter how long I struggle to solve the word puzzle or the sudoku puzzle, I can know that there's a solution and if I can stay with it long enough (even if I must walk away from it for a while - which is actually a brilliant idea when you get stuck), that solution will become apparent to me. And in that light, I never get frustrated.
I only get curious.

So today, whatever "problems" may arise for you, re-MIND yourself, the solution is there and if you keep your mind right (enthusiasm) you'll find it sooner than later.

Here's a healthy invitation for you for today:

Make extremely good EYE CONTACT - with a smile - with EVERYONE with whom you come in contact.

It's so simple and can be so profoundly enriching, and yet has become so easy to avoid and even awkward or EVEN deemed creepy or inappropriate.

Try it.

Really good, solid eye contact, with a smile - even with complete strangers. An see if you co-create some magic with "only" that.

Over the last 30 years since Gallup started this particular poll, 84% of Americans have reported disliking their jobs. Let that soak in for a sec.

That means about 1.5 people out of 10 DO like their jobs. That's mind-blowing. And I interpret it to mean one thing: the vast majority of people are settling because they believe they must.

The life you want is what you're designed for, and nothing less. Not just with respect to your career, with your LIFE.

How might you be settling?

I love asking myself that question.

There are very very few of us who aren't settling in some way.

How are you settling, and what can you do TODAY to stop?

I saw an ad for Disneyland yesterday. The music they used was that song from Pinocchio, "When You Wish Upon a Star." Do you know the lyrics? "When you wish upon a star....anything your heart desires will come to you." Now let me preface this roast by saying that I LOVE what Walt Disney was about and I love Disney World and I love that it's nickname is the Magic Kingdom and all the great metaphors there are for how magical life is. But that song, that shit's weak. Wish upon a star? That's like the movie, The Secret. Stupid. Say your affirmations and the universe will provide. That ain't how it works. What if YOU ARE THE UNIVERSE? Then you gotta do the providing, don't you? The co-creating. Excellence has NEVER come from setting affirmations or intentions all day. The Mentally Tough get that. The intent initiates the immediate, bold and masterful action - ACTION that YOU take. And the repetition of that over and over and over is what creates the miracles. So forget about this wishing nonsense. You are the entire universe pretending to be human. Co-create miracles.

Mental Toughness is having a mind
that is trained to respond to unpredictable
circumstances in precisely the way you wished
you'd respond and that you feel proud of.

But instead of having to wait for
lots of surprises in order to train,
you can fabricate them in your mind's eye.

Take some circumstances or events from your
memory - one's that you wished you'd responded
to with much more mastery, and visualize yourself
responding perfectly. Perfectly.

Do it over and over and over. These are
repetitions. Just like the reps you do in a set of
pushups in a workout.

Accumulate the reps and you get gains!

Here's a cool Mental Toughness Tool for the day. It's called either "The Warrior's Code" or "Dying Before Going into Battle."

Samurai Warriors would convince themselves before heading into a battle that they'd already died, so there was absolutely nothing to fear. Nothing to hold back for. Nothing to avoid. So they were totally free and needless. And could thus go ALL IN!

You can use this same mentality before going into a negotiation, a proposal, an offer, a performance review or any other event in your life that's important to you.

Tell yourself beforehand (in your pre-game routine) that you need nothing from this person or these people. Nothing. You literally need nothing. Then you can go in without distraction and be the ultimate courageous you.

Mental Toughness reminder for today:

Listen deeply.

Permit yourself to relinquish the need to formulate responses when the other is speaking.

Do not interrupt. At all.

In fact, even create pauses after they've finished and before your response. Enjoy the uniqueness of impeccable listening today.

**Daydreaming is powerful.**

**No matter what you're envisioning, you are unconsciously creating that. So today be very MIND-FULL to fill your mind with images of all that could go right. Exceptionally right.**

Today's Mental Toughness invitation is to blame
NO ONE and NO THING for your emotions.

Take complete ownership of
every single state that you think your way into.

Did you catch that?

You think your way into every state you ever
experience, so how could anything outside of you
ever be responsible for how you feel?

*"Worry is a misuse of the imagination."*

That's a quote from my former coach, Steve Chandler. And I couldn't agree more.

So today's challenge is to catch yourself when you're worrying about anything and switch your attention to what's wonerful and what beauty is possible for you.

All forms of training involve reps, or repetitions of exercises. Same for Mental Toughness Training.

So many - if not most - of these Daily Doses are quite similar in nature. I want to revisit the power of your vibe this morning.

We're always vibing and our vibe either empowers us or weakens us. This is measurable.

So today,
instead of bringing donuts
to the meeting (literally or metaphorically),
bring the vibe.

Take a few moments before you
interact with folks today to get your vibe high
by thinking your way into a state of cooperation,
collaboration, solution focused thinking and
compassion and connectedness.

So instead of waiting to see how the vibe is,
YOU be the bearer of the high vibe and
invite everyone else to join you there.

Shame is very possibly the most toxic of emotions that we think ourselves into.

And it's all learned.

Which is good news.
Because we can unlearn it.

And here's a must faster approach
to doing that than intellectualizing it -
which we've also learned to do.

LOVE it. Honestly.

When you catch yourself feeling shame, remove all resistance to it. What we resist persists, so don't resist. Rather, literally love it.

Your truth is divine - perfect. What could ever be wrong with your truth?! So love the shame and then with respect to the thing your were ashamed of, tell yourself it's simply a behavior you choose not to repeat. Let that be your standard response to shame. And watch it fade away into serenity.

That's some serious Mental Toughness right there.

So many of us are governed by the learned need to be right and to have people approve of us.

Take a moment right now to imagine what life is like in the absolute absense of the need to prove anything (unless you're a lawyer, but you know what I mean, in your personal life).

No need to do any of that work. Imagine that.

How easy and light that is. Today, experiment with fully relinquishing the need to prove anything.

This Daily Dose is about the process. That is to say, the process of all these practices and disciplines that I write about in here.

I am certain that I get as much value as anyone - if not more - by doing the work to craft these messages. This has become a wonderful part of my own Mental Toughness Training practice.

Each one of these messages is a reminder to myself to freshen, or continue or sometimes to re-engage these practices that I may have forgotten about or abandoned over time.

I am my first client and I practice these tools myself. I will not share something unless I have practiced it deeply.

And the operative word there is practice. As Allen Iverson once said, "We're talking 'bout practice!"

## What does perfect look like?

This is one of the most powerful questions you can ask yourself - and answer in detail - prior to any kind of performance.

If you're in sales, take a moment prior to your client/prospect call, your forecast call, your performance review and visualize yourself being masterful.

If you're an athlete, visualize perfection prior to the competition as well as each shot or serve or kick.

If you're a student taking a test, see yourself in your mind's eye having perfect access to recall and problem solving.

If you're about to have a conversation with your spouse about a disagreement, experience yourself prior to it being a perfect, compassionate listener.

A little pre-work in the mind goes a long way.

Here's another question that I find quite useful as a guide on how to show up right now:

*"How will I want to speak about this moment when I'm on my death bed?"*

In other words,
who do I need to be right now in order to
show up in a way that I will be quite proud of?

Some folks really have a hard time with being told to "loosen up." They take offense to it. I love it.

I think it's a great reminder. I can't think of a time when loosening up either physically, mentally or both has not served me well.

We take ourselves so seriously.

Loose and light today. That's the plan.

**REMINDER:**

One of the most valuable
questions for a human to entertain is:

*"How can I serve?"*

Let that inquiry be your North Star today.

Here's a great Mental Toughness rule of thumb.

Whenever you're feeling unpleasant, ever,
it is simply because in that moment
you are believing a thought that's not true.

For simplicity's sake, we can generalize that most
of those times you could reduce your experience
in that moment to the phrase, "This sucks."
And that could never be proven.
It is merely a low grade interpretation.

And you always possess the ability to rewrite that
story or upgrade that interpretation and decide
that your truth is much more inspiring.

Catch the lies today and upgrade.

In your mind, unlike on American Airlines,
there are unlimited free upgrades available to you
always. Use them.

In our fast paced lives,
we forget to breathe correctly.

Take a deep abdominal breath right now.

A nice big full breath all the way into your abdomine. And release it fully and loudly. That's all it takes to oxygenate your muscles and relax.

Breathe well today.

From Eastern Philosophy comes many
a solid Mental Toughness practice.

One of them is non-attachment. Everything in this
world is impermanent. Like King Solomon's ring
said, "This too shall pass."

And that refers to everything. Every mood will
pass. The great ones as well as the dark ones.
Every day will pass. Every one of us will pass.

So we have two options, cling frantically to what
is, or surrender peacefully into the impermanence.

Clinging is prison. Non-attachment is freedom.

Let's revisit one of your most powerful Mental Toughness Tools in the toolbox today:

Game Face.

Your Game Face is the mood you're in when you're at your best.

Do you know yours?

If not, think back to an event where you were truly crushing it. Recall a peak performance and then answer this: How'd you feel emotionally?

What was your state as you were kicking ass? Come up with three words that accurately capture that remarkably powerful state and before performing from now on, take a moment and get into that state in advance.

Don't WAIT for amazing results to feel great. Flip that. Feel amazing and then create amazing results from that.

Create the state; don't wait!

Warren Buffet said,

*"Investing in yourself is the best investment you'll ever make in your life... There's no financial investment that'll ever match it, because if you develop more skill, more ability, more insight, more capacity, that's what's going to really provide economic freedom."*

And I'll add emotional freedom to that. Which has no price tag and infinite value.

How can you upgrade the ways that you invest in your own growth these days?

The number ONE mistake that I have made, and my clients have made in the pursuit of our dreams is waiting.

Peter Thiel, co-founder of PayPal, when asked what he wished he'd known about business 20 years ago, said,

*"I wish I would have known that there was no need to wait. So if you're planning to do something with your life, and you have a 10 year plan of how to get there, you should ask: Why can't you do this in 6 months? Sometimes you have to go the full 10 year trajectory, but it's at least worth asking whether that's the story you're telling yourself or whether that's the reality."*

I always want to assume that my timeline projections are way off that way.
And I'm happy to be wrong.

Here's a great quote from Mark Twain:

*"I am an old man and I have known a great many troubles, but most of them never happened."*

There is only one place in the universe where "problems" exist. In the human mind.

Have today's practice be to catch yourself feeling troubled, and see if you can turn it around into some inspiration.

Operate from the "Life is happening FOR me" attitude today vs. it's happening "to me."

Create some magic from that place.

A few years ago when I was in a really dark place emotionally and I was having trouble getting out of bed, not to mention out of my shitty self pity, I made a profound discovery.

I was tired of trying to upgrade my thoughts so I decided to get out of "me" an get into doing something kind for someone else.

I literally left my own world and departed to go shopping for a nice tequila for a friend who really loves tequila (I was in Mexico at the time so this was convenient). I shifted completely and started elevating. Compassion transforms pain.

An untrained mind will likely hear with great skepticism the suggestion that excellence can be created from every set of circumstances.

The untrained mind might say something like, "That's just some rose-colored glasses, silver lining, glass half full crap." And that's what our conditioning would have us believe.

The trained mind, however, realizes that every situation is truly loaded with potential and that potential will only be realized with masterful interpretations.

The problem is the gift.
Practice seeing it that way today.

Here's an amazing, completely practical tool for reprogramming habitual crappy responses to reality. When you catch yourself blurting out crap like, "This traffic sucks!" finish that off by adding to it, "Unless it doesn't."

You're coming out of a meeting where some weird decisions were made and you say to yourself, or someone else, "This is bullshit." Add to it, "Unless it isn't."

This is a remarkably effective method of interrupting mindless, low-grade reactions that deactivate intelligence and cut you off from creative genius.

After a while, you'll notice that you'll skip the complaint/problem part and jump right up into the creativity/possibility mindset.

That's Mental Toughness.

When people ask how I'm doing I often reply by saying, "This is the best damn day of my life." And sometimes they think I'm insincere about that. But I'm never insincere about that.

Once in a while someone will reply with, "Wow. What happened?" And I say "I chose it to be." And that's the message.

We don't ever need to wait for anything unusually spectacular to occur in order to decide that this is the best day of our lives.

In fact, I'd argue that the probability of something spectacular happening increases with such a decision to elevate state first.

Choose this to be the best day of your life. Until tomorrow.

How do you most profoundly want to
use the rest of your life?

Boom! How's THAT for a doozie of a question?!

I first heard that articulated by one of my favorite
teachers in history, the late Dr. Wayne Dyer.

Note the language. It doesn't say, "What do you
want to do for a living?" Or even, "What do you
want to DO with the rest of your life?"

It says "profoundly" and "use" - those are the
operative words. Reflect on that question.

I used that question this morning in a coaching
session. And I ask myself that question often,
knowing full well that my truth can change over
time. But it is a hugely important question that
most people never consider.

Profound USE of this miraculous life.
Whattaya say?

Present moment awareness is such a huge tool/skill/practice in Mental Toughness Training.

Unpleasant emotions cannot exist when we are fully present in this moment.

Shame and anger and regret exist only in thoughts of the past. Fear exists only in thoughts of a disastrous future. There's only peace and heightened focus in the present.

There are a ton of different exercies to practice bringing yourself back to now, here's one of them:

Count the number of different shades of green that you can see right now. Even if there are no green hues visible at the moment, in the moments that you are looking for them you experience no regret, no shame, no anger, no fear or anxiety of any form. There is only serenity. Notice that.

You can always bring yourself instantly back into the peacefulness of this one moment.

Just saw a post from one of my good buddies, an amazing author and speaker and coach, and A-Fest host/MC, Jason Goldberg. (Look him up and follow his stuff!)

He was talking about "beginner's luck." Which is a fascinating thing, isn't it? He goes on to say that such "luck" is always available if you have what's called "beginner's mind." Shoshin (初心) is a word from Zen Buddhism meaning "beginner's mind."

It refers to having an attitude of openness, eagerness, and lack of preconceptions when studying a subject, even when studying at an advanced level, just as a beginner would.

I took a friend golfing for her first time ever several years ago. Her ball went into a greenside sand bunker. I briefly instructed her on how to hit the shot by aggressively digging the club into the sand an inch behind the ball with a full swing and follow through. She hit the ball to two feet of the hole! It was almost perfect. Because she hadn't learned yet how "hard" it is to do that.

There is great intelligence in fun.

I like to say that fun is one of the most responsible things you can ever do. I also ridicule the phrase, "There's a time for work and a time for play." I think that is absurdly stupid.

Because if you look at any human peak performance research, you will NEVER find an instance of someone in the zone who described the experience as effortful.

Isn't that fascinating?!

Instead people always describe their peak performances as the opposite - effortless.

And fun.

So, do not go to "work" today.
Go to "fun" today. Even if at work.

In my Mental Toughness Training I talk about "Outcome Decisions" and "Process Decisions."

An Outcome Decision could be, we WILL win the National Championship this season.

A Process Decision for that would be, I am going to make this practice today the best practice I have ever had.

If I am willing to commit fully to the process day in and day out with the same degree of passion that I have for the final outcome, not only do I maximize the probability of success, but I also grow a million times stronger and love the getting there immeasurably more.

You've heard the term "self talk," right?
It's kind of a big deal.

We're always talking to ourselves.

If you could get a transcript of your inner dialog
from yesterday, you might be aghast at how
unpleasantly you spoke to yourself.

If you were to speak to your loved ones that way,
you'd likely lose a lot of relationships.

So today, let's be acutely aware of our self talk
and have it be like the language you'd want an
amazing coach to use with you. Maybe not always
complimentary, but always in absolute support.

I think it would be a disservice for me to not remind you every so often of the immense power of and intelligence in the state of gratitude.

Hear this as if for the very first time.

Gratitude is always available to you (as is every state). Gratitude activates all forms of intelligence. Gratitude nourishes you and connects us.

Dedicate today to gratitude.

Set a few notifications for gratitude reminders in your phone and when they go off, take a few moments and express gratitude both inwardly and outwardly for the beauty and the excellence an the greatness that is in your world.

## Quiz time!

### Where does confidence come from?

Think it through. (That was a subtle hint.) Think about it. (Less subtle.) You got it! It comes from THINKING! It does NOT come from good results.

We all have known classmates who always got straight A's but still worried endlessly about tests.

If it were true that good results produced confidence, then that would never happen. Ever.

What are the thoughts that you think to yourself when you're feeling totally confident? Think them non-stop today. Create unprecedented levels of confidence today.

Form. Good form.

Actually perfect form. Perfect form is powerful.

How can you practice perfect form today?
Exercise? Posture? Driving? Listening? Self talk?
Writing? Speaking? The ways are endless.

Dedicate today to perfect form.

Here's a really tough Mental Toughness Training challenge for you today. Pay VERY close attention all day to when you avoid or compromise your truth for fear of how it will sound to the other(s).

This is a toughie because the ego is sooooo sneaky that it'll be justifying it as you're doing it!

We have all been conditioned to be self-conscious about our truths.

One of the greatest lessons I learned in my work in India at The Oneness University was that there could never be anything wrong with your truth.

So heighten your awareness today to the times when you are self-conscious.

That alone is great training.

Another tough Mental Toughness challenge for you my friend. (Two in a row, I know!)

Think of situations in which you get defensive (a low grade response to reality that masters do not choose).

Next, imagine how you'd love to respond in those situations.

Next, go CREATE those situations, put yourself in the scenery where they are very likely to occur.

And finally, after it's over, if you didn't love the way you responded, do some mental do-overs imagining yourself responding purely masterfully.

This is how we create rapid deep growth reps. This stuff is more powerful than burpees!!!

Walk into it today.

Walk into what?

Walk into the ideal you.

Just like it's Halloween and you're going as the ultra-badass you. Talk that way. Walk that way. Decide that way. Take some risks that will have your ego tell you, "Yo, Dude, they're gonna think you're cocky! Slow your role!"

Who and how would you be today
if you weren't allowed to be afraid?

Operate from the assumption today,
that when your mind is telling you
that you're out of juice,
it's wrong.

When I'm coaching a golfer on Mental Toughness and they ask what they should be thinking right before they execute the swing or the stroke, I tell them ideally you're thoughtless.

But that is quite difficult unless you have practiced a lot of Transcendental Meditation.

So if you haven't strengthened that skill, the next best thing is to simply think the words, "yes" and "good" repeatedly.

We have such strong positive associations with those words that merely thinking them to ourselves elevates our state. As I'm sure you can see, this isn't only useful for golfers.

Tony Robbins once asked Nelson Mandela how he survived all those years in prison. Mandela replied,

*"I didn't survive - I prepared."*

He utilized the circumstance.
That's Mental Toughness.

And he happened to utilize the situation to serve humanity. That's mastery. ALL circumstances can be utilized for good. Remember that today.

Punctuality is an expression of Mental Toughness. It is an expression of integrity. Tardiness is weak. It is a power leak. It's almost always avoidable.

If you habitually run late for things, stop it!

Make time to sit down and take a really good look at the way you schedule your life and the ways that you use your time.

Examine that closely and make changes so that you aren't always in a harried rush. Slowing down has been the most lucrative discipline in my life.

Paradoxically, slowing down with my appointment making has sped up a lot of good things.

Consider someone who self-reportedly takes things personally often. If you asked them why is that and they said, "It's just how I am" - that could never be true.

What could be true is that that is how they have historically behaved.

We have been conditioned to believe that certain behaviors or personality characteristics are genetic and therefore static (and even epigenetics now dismantles the notion that even our genes are static, so even if a trait like short-temperedness was genetic, it can be manipulated).

Say your father had a bad temper. And you have also demonstrated a similar short fuse, it's not how or who you are. It's how you behave and you can always manipulate that.

What if it was true
that every problem you ever experienced
was an ingeniously and purposefully crafted
challenge offered to you by an intelligent and
loving universe that is fully in support of you,
wants you to evolve, and knows that that is what
you are designed for?

If that feels inspiring, then go with that. In fact,
always do that - always go with what feels
inspiring.

Here's a cool brain training exercise that involves heightening your awareness of thought content (which, of course, is a pre-requisite to manipulating your thoughts).

Close your eyes and ask yourself,

*"What will my next thought be?"*

Then, like a cat staring at a mouse hole, watch. You don't even have to do anything with the thought that comes out of that hole.

Just notice it.

Now, for extra credit, if the thought sucks, then you can go ahead and upgrade it.

Providence is an interesting term.

I never use that word (unless Villanova Men's Basketball is playing against Providence College), but I just read it somewhere and I like it.

Providence is like synchronicity. Or the organizing intelligence. Or God. In any event, it sure seems to be true that when I fully commit to something, then Providence kicks in.

Like Paulo Coehlo writes in his famous book, The Alchemist - the universe conspires to assist you.

Fully commit to something important to you this morning. And then greet Providence when it shows up.

I've said it time and time again, and I just saw it in
about 3 different books that I'm reading,
Gratefulness is one of the most highly intelligent
states to choose to think yourself into. It activates
all forms of intelligence, including creative genius.

Create a lot of gratitude today.

I am always talking about
upgrading your thought content so you can
upgrade your emotional experience.

One of the mistakes that is often made in Mental
Toughness Training is the notion that there are
evil or inappropriate thoughts and that they must
be fought and condemned! That's nonsense.

That's giving WAY too much power to these little
things that are simply, and absolutely nothing
more than, thoughts. "Oooooh how I'd like to beat
the shit out that jackwagon!" Is that a sinful
thought? Is it despicable and warped?
No. It's nothing more than a damn thought.
Acting on it would be dark and hurtful.
But the thought itself is simply a thought.

So if you ever think to yourself something like,
"OMG, what is WRONG with me for having these
horrible thoughts?!" you can just go ahead and
relieve yourself of all of that judgment.
And from now on you can simply follow up the
funky thought with the thought, "Ain't no thing but
a chicken wing! Just a thought."

In his book, The Four Agreements,
Don Miguel Ruiz includes being impeccable with
your word as one of the agreements.

And I have noticed that
in my efforts to be impeccable with my word,
my intent is nowhere near enough.

My intent to keep my word is simply the first step
in the process of doing what it takes to ENSURE
that I keep my word.

I am taking great avantage of modern technology
to assist me in being impeccable. I send myself a
lot of messages and reminders and alerts. I want
to treat my word as it should be treated - the
strongest contract on the planet.

What else can you do in order to
be impeccable with your word?

Do you know what an "Aha moment" is?

It's that moment in time when you discover the solution to a puzzle or a challenge that has been eluding you. AHA!!!

These are enormously powerful moments. These are moments of consciousness expansion (that term is synonymous with Mental Toughness).

An aha moment is a moment of true growth. It's one of the (several) reasons I do puzzles every day. I want to create as many aha's as possible.

So pay attention to when you go, "Oh!" and "Aha!" And absorb the feeling that accompanies that expansive experience. It's a cool one and it's a good one to spend more time in.

As humans, we are designed for growth.

Every bit of effort you invest in developing yourself has profound, and usually invisible, effects on MANY other people.

That is, at minimum, part of your contribution to global transformation.

I assume you are reading this because you are committed to your own growth. And that makes the world a better place for ME, so THANK YOU!

I'd like to remind you that the odds of you happening are incomprehensibly improbable.

That makes you a miracle by definition.

You are a 1 in 10 to the 2.7 millionth power likelihood. That math was done by a Harvard Professor. That seems to me to be cause to celebrate the simple and profound fact that you are alive.

Have a miraculous day, you Miracle!

Made in the USA
Middletown, DE
30 June 2019